Profitability and Law Firm Management

Profitability and Law Firm Management

SECOND EDITION

Andrew Otterburn

The Law Society

ISBN 978 1 85328 598 1

Published in 2007 by the Law Society
113 Chancery Lane, London WC2A 1PL

Typeset by J&L Composition, Filey, North Yorkshire
Printed by TJ International Ltd, Padstow, Cornwall

To
Debbie, Joanna and Samuel

Contents

About the author

Andrew Otterburn is a chartered accountant and management consultant, and has been advising solicitors since 1989.

He was Grant Thornton's senior legal consultant for a number of years and was instrumental in setting up their Legal Business Group. He set up his own firm in 1996 and, together with his colleague Dr Heather Stewart, advises law firms on their profitability, management and future direction. He also undertakes a considerable amount of management training each year.

Since 1989 he has advised around 250 firms of solicitors across the UK and in Ireland. He is co-author of the annual Survey of Legal Practices in Scotland and since 2003 has conducted an annual benchmarking survey of firms in Ireland. In 2006 he was an advisor to Lord Carter's Review of Legal Aid Procurement.

Preface

The law is in a constant state of change – it always has been and is always likely to be. What has changed over the last decade is the degree of change that has taken place within the legal system itself – ranging from the structures and management styles of firms, through the way the market operates, to the way individual lawyers actually do their work. Much has changed since 1998 when I wrote my first book for the Law Society.

At the time of writing this new edition, in the spring of 2007, it is clear that the pace of change is accelerating and that the whole landscape of the profession is about to change. Four factors in particular will drive this change:

- the impact of the internet on workflows;
- the Legal Services Bill, in particular its provisions for new entrants to the legal market and the external ownership of law firms;
- commoditisation;
- Lord Carter's review of Legal Aid Procurement.

The first three are likely to impact in particular on firms that derive significant amounts of work from private clients – the traditional 'high street' firm – and also corporate players. The latter is likely to have a big effect on the 2,000 or so firms that still undertake publicly funded work.

The legal landscape in 1998 was populated by City firms; a number of strong provincial firms, often single office, drawing much of their work from within their region; and a large number of smaller firms undertaking private client, commercial and legally aided work. Today the City firms are international organisations, often with strong US links; the provincial firms of 1998 invariably now have City offices or have become national players, and the number of firms undertaking legal aid has halved. The bulk of the profession still comprises the many smaller firms that provide a mix of private client and commercial work.

In five years' time, by 2012, I suspect the legal landscape will have changed significantly. It is likely to be populated by a smaller number of larger firms, and niche players. There will be half as many firms again undertaking legal aid, and generally they will be larger. Much private client work currently undertaken by 'high street' firms, in particular residential conveyancing, will be provided by larger organisations in 'legal factories' – perhaps owned by banks or membership organisations, but also owned by law firms. Tesco law will have arrived, although Tesco itself may not be one of the providers.

As always during any period of change the winners will be those that are able to adapt in a changing environment.

For some areas of law, having excellent lawyers will be critical, but for many firms it will be useful but not essential. Having well-motivated and businesslike people able to work in and lead teams is likely to be more important. Effective business skills, an ability to spot and take advantage of opportunities and an ability to plan, manage and lead a firm are likely to be more important, along with effective financial management.

This book concentrates on England and Wales, but also draws on the experience of firms in Scotland and Ireland. At the time of writing this edition a growing number of firms had converting to LLP (Limited Liability Partnership) status, however most were still partnerships. For simplicity in this edition I have continued therefore to refer generally to the situation facing partnerships. Members of an LLP should find it relatively straightforward to equate the points being made to their circumstances.

Once again, this book tries not simply to indicate what to do, but to provide some tips on how to do it. It is not intended to be the definitive or only way of doing things, but is designed to help partners and others involved in practice management think about their firms and identify ways of making them more successful. Its purpose is once again to help you move forward.

> **Andrew Otterburn**
> **Holmfirth**
> **May 2007**

Acknowledgements

As in my previous two books I would like to thank the many people who have contributed quotes and comments for inclusion in this book. In particular I would like to thank my clients and the many people I meet at seminars. They, hopefully, learn from me, but I always learn from them.

I would like to thank the people who have contributed the case studies at the end of each chapter in the first two sections for contributing their thoughts and being willing to waive confidentiality.

I would once again like to acknowledge the work of the many Law Society staff I have worked with in recent years for the contribution and initiative they have shown in helping firms improve the management of their practices. These are the people who often come up with the good ideas and work hard to see them through. In particular, I would like to thank Maureen Miller and Marga Auz.

I would also like to thank: the Law Management Section for allowing me to re-analyse and use their Financial Benchmarking Survey 2005; and Bruce Ritchie of the Law Society of Scotland for allowing me to use charts from the 2006 Survey of Legal Practices in Scotland.

1

Developing the business in a fast changing world

What is changing

Clementi, Carter and the Legal Services Bill – structural change in England and Wales

The legal profession is entering a period of significant change – in particular in England and Wales.

The report by Sir David Clementi in December 2004 on the provision of legal services and the government's subsequent publication of the Legal Services Bill in 2006 setting out its proposals for the regulatory reform of legal services marked the start of a period of significant change for the profession in England and Wales. There are regulatory changes that will impact on the professional bodies, but arguably of greater importance to practitioners are the wide-ranging changes that will impact on individual firms. In particular:

- **Employed solicitors being allowed to act direct for the public** – enabling organisations (for example, a membership organisation such as the RAC, a bank, or perhaps an insurance company) to set up a law firm and provide services direct to their members or to the public. Such organisations are likely to be very selective about the services they provide, and are likely to offer them in a highly com-moditised environment – such as out-of-town business parks with high levels of investment in IT and systems. They are likely to be well structured with work being done in well supervised teams, rarely by qualified lawyers.
- **The possibility of different business models** – enabling partnership with not just other legal professionals, as recommended by Sir David, but also other members of non-legal professions, as set out in the Bill. It is not clear at this stage how much interest there is in multi-disciplinary practices, and certainly the accountants who entered the law in the late 1990s do not seem to be showing interest. This provision may, however, permit the finance, HR, marketing, IT and other professionals who increasingly play a key part in the manage-ment of firms to enter partnership. The possibility of entering into partnership with barristers or legal executives will also be attractive to many firms.

- **Alternative business structures** (ABSs) – will permit ownership of a law firm, or investment by external investors.

Competition has increased even before the Bill has been enacted, resulting in changed workflows and patterns of working. There is a clear move amongst some existing law firms to anticipate the changes that are coming and ensure they are ahead of the game. In particular, in residential conveyancing, there is a move towards referrals in bulk to panel firms from banks or internet-based referral agencies. The referrals are to firms with the IT and systems to process them in volume and who are able to compete effectively on price. The same is true for re-mortgage work and some areas of personal injury.

For many high street firms, residential conveyancing is still an important part of their fee income, and there must be a real concern that this will be increasingly referred to panels of firms by referral agencies. As in the case of personal injury work over the last decade, traditional 'off the street' and 'own client' work may decline, to be replaced with clients instructing new bulk providers, perhaps owned by lenders.

For firms that undertake publicly funded work, the summer of 2006 saw the publication of the long-awaited report by Lord Carter on legal aid procurement. The impact of this will be as far-reaching for the firms that still undertake legal aided work as that of Sir David for the profession as a whole. The report by Lord Carter visualised a move towards a smaller number of larger firms undertaking work increasingly on a fixed or competitive fee basis. The emphasis will once again be on systems, use of technology and work being done at an appropriate level.

Justice 2 Committee and the Personal Injuries Assessment Board – structural change in Scotland and Ireland

Whilst the Clementi report only directly affected England and Wales its effects are likely to be felt over time in other jurisdictions such as Scotland and Ireland. At the time of writing, the profession in Scotland was coming to terms with Clementi-style reforms to regulation following recommendations by the Justice 2 Committee of the Scottish Parliament, and the Competition Authority in Ireland had published a report that could lead to Clementi-style change in the Republic.

Procedural changes introduced by the government in Ireland led to the virtual collapse of the personal injury market following the introduction of the Personal Injuries Assessment Board (PIAB) in 2003. This had a direct impact on the market for residential conveyancing as personal injury solicitors tried to diversify into other areas, in particular conveyancing, to compensate for the loss of personal injury fees. PIAB had the initial effect of significantly reducing the income of personal injury firms, and this is likely to persist. For many smaller firms, personal injury and residential conveyancing are the mainstays of their income, so the effect of PIAB has been significant. The result has been diversification and a sudden need to adopt more focused business and marketing strategies – something new for a majority of firms. The immediate reaction of many firms had been to cut their fees for residential conveyancing, so as to obtain additional work, and the overall result has been a squeeze on profitability.

The bottom line is that in each jurisdiction competition has increased, and in particular price competition is becoming ever more important. As ever, when a market undergoes a significant period of change there is a need to plan, and the key is to be thinking about the issues before the impending changes rather than afterwards, when it is often too late. Forward planning enables firms to take advantage of the opportunities. A failure properly to plan can easily leave firms having to respond to changes which by then have become a threat.

IT, the internet and commoditisation

Underlying, and making possible, much of the change in recent years have been developments in IT, communications and the internet.

In 1998 many lawyers[1] did not have a computer on their desks, and many who did have one had it on a side desk where it did not interfere with their work. They tended to use computers primarily to ascertain balances on client accounts or to make accounts enquiries. It was not integral to their work. It was for their secretaries and it was for the accounts department, but it was incidental to their own work.

By 2007 the position had changed completely, and that process of change is likely to accelerate. Improved communications now allow firms to outsource typing and some back office functions to other cities or to other countries, in particular India. The service can be just as good, sometimes better, and the cost lower. One of the leading Bristol firms was able to use time differences to competitive advantage through arrangements with firms in New Zealand who could undertake initial work on documents overnight so as to speed turnaround the following day when the lawyers in Bristol could complete the work. Such working methods would not have been possible back in the mid 1990s.

New entrants to the market and growing price competition, combined with advances in technology, have resulted in greater commoditisation of legal services. The result is that services previously regarded as bespoke, that would have been provided by solicitors, are being undertaken by more junior staff, not always qualified, using case management and knowledge management systems. Life is changing and the pace of change is likely to accelerate over the next decade.

Globalisation and its impact on commercial firms

Since 1998 the major commercial firms in both London and cities in other parts of the UK have also seen significant change in their markets and practices.

The key change has been the demand from multinational clients for firms that can represent their interests globally 24 hours a day, and the consequent development of a number of significant international practices. There has been a concentration of clients and work amongst a small number of ever-larger firms, and the market has become ever more competitive. The leading City firms that were large in 1998 have now become global. The Lawyer Global 100[2] places three UK firms – Clifford Chance, Linklaters and Freshfields Bruckhaus Deringer – in the top five international firms, with fees of around £1 billion each, and together these three firms employ more than 6,500 lawyers worldwide.

As business has become more international and clients have clustered around a smaller number of mega firms, the pressure has increased on mid-sized firms. Some mid-sized City firms have merged with US firms in order to maintain and enhance their competitive position, or have established international networks of offices, or strategic alliances. Increasingly there is a need for these firms to be larger.

These mid-sized firms have also increasingly sought work from clients who might previously have been served by provincial firms. This has increased pressure on the provincial commercial firms, many of whom have, in response, opened offices in London.

All-round competition has become more intense and there has been a need for these larger firms also to evolve.

What might the profession look like in, say, 2012?

As discussed earlier in this chapter, the profession in England and Wales is likely to change significantly over the five years between 2007 and 2012, and life is also likely to be different for lawyers in Scotland and Ireland. The change ahead will affect firms differently depending on the types of work they undertake, the markets they operate in, their location, size and the ability and skill of their senior managers.

In 2005 there were approximately 9,000 firms in England and Wales, as summarised in Table 1.1. The table indicates the total number of solicitors and the average number of solicitors for each size group. The table suggests the total number of lawyers there might be in an average firm in each size group.

Table 1.1 indicates that the vast majority of firms were relatively small, with fewer than five solicitors, many of whom were partners. Just

Table 1.1 The profession in 2005

Number of partners	Number of firms	Total number of solicitors	Solicitors per firm	Total lawyers per firm*
1	4,200	6,500	1.5	3
2–4	3,600	17,400	5	10
5–10	800	12,500	16	30
11–25	300	12,000	40	80
26–80	100	12,400	124	250
81+	30	17,300	575	1,150
TOTAL	9,030	78,100		

Source: Law Society – Annual Statistical Report 2005

*It is assumed that on average there is one lawyer in addition to each solicitor

14% of firms had more than five partners, although these firms accounted for the vast majority of solicitors in the profession.

Historically, small firms have often been very successful; indeed it was the business model that developed during the latter part of the twentieth century that was most appropriate to the markets most firms in the UK operated in. A key question is, what is the most appropriate business model likely to be in the future?

It is quite possible that over the next five years:

- a significant amount of residential conveyancing will move from traditional high street firms to bulk operations – perhaps 50%, possibly less – but it could be higher if the experience of personal injury is a guide;
- there will be far fewer firms undertaking legal aid – perhaps 50%;
- commercial firms will have continued to get larger;
- services will be delivered in an ever more cost-effective way – competition will demand it, and for many this will mean greater team working and better use of IT.

Over time, as the profession evolves, it may well become clear that the new business model that firms will need to work towards is one that is much larger than at present.

The days of a firm having just one or two lawyers undertaking, for example, family work or conveyancing are likely to be nearing an end. Small teams, in particular if they contain relatively senior lawyers, tend to be expensive. In Part III below, the concept of hourly cost is discussed, but the evidence would suggest that team working results in more competitive hourly costs. Teams of five or six – or more – lawyers may become the norm. They will include a team leader (who will not necessarily be a partner), two or three solicitors and perhaps four or five other lawyers – a team of six to 10 people.

On the basis that most firms will probably undertake four or five areas of work, it is very easy to visualise practices with around 30–50 lawyers – not the firms with fewer than 10 lawyers seen so often at present.

These firms are likely to:

- be single site – there will be far fewer branch offices unless they are in different towns;
- be in modern, open-plan buildings – buildings that make team working much easier, that aid communications and that are much easier for cabling;
- invest heavily in IT;
- make much greater use of professional managers.

There will still be some small firms, in particular specialist practices, and many sole practitioners, but these will increasingly be experienced principals who have left a larger firm to set up on their own. They are likely to be 'niche', and will offer experience and expertise.

SUMMARY

- **The next five years from 2007 to 2012 is likely to be a period of significant change as a result of the Legal Services Bill and legal aid reform.**
- **There are likely to be changes in workflows away from traditional high street firms towards larger factory operations.**
- **Commercial firms are likely to see continuing change as a result of globalisation that is likely to see an ever greater need for size.**
- **Over the next five years there is likely to be consolidation amongst smaller firms and the development of a new business model that works – very probably one that is much larger than the one that exists in 2007.**
- **There will be a smaller number of large single-office firms.**

Notes

1   In this edition the generic term 'lawyer' is generally used instead of 'fee earner'. The latter is still widely used within the profession, however some firms have banned its use as it was also being used in correspondence with clients.
2   See **www.thelawyer.com**.

Joy Kingsley, managing partner – Pannone LLP, Manchester

How long have you been managing partner for?	15 years.
How many partners and lawyers does your firm have?	350
How would you describe your firm (top 100, high street, publicly funded etc. . .)?	Top 100 full service.
What percentage of your time is spent on management?	100%
How did you find your first few months as managing partner?	Can't remember!
What are the best parts of the job?	Success – shaping the future for yourself and your firm.
What are the hardest parts of the job?	Managing other partners and dealing with government intervention.
How do you balance fee earning with management?	N/a
Any tips on motivating fellow partners and providing leadership?	Spend time with all partners as individuals. Work harder than your partners and remain positive.
How do you see the role of departmental/team leaders?	Departmental leaders motivate partners and troops to follow a business and marketing plan, provide client service etc. They work in partnership with the managing partner to produce strength across all the departments in support of the overarching principles and branding of the firm.
What qualities would you look for in your successor?	Drive, ambition, ability and a wish to work hard. People and motivational skills. Decision making skills. Entrepreneurial skills.

What advice would you give your successor?	Don't take yourself too seriously; motivate your partners; don't isolate yourself; and build something different to me.
Would you consider a non-lawyer chief executive as your successor?	No.
Any other thoughts?	There are many ways to make it work.

2

The need for a plan

Why plan?

The degree of change that is likely to hit the profession over the next three to five years from 2007 means that, more so than ever before, firms need to have a plan – a robust business strategy that will help them adapt, and successfully respond to the challenges that lie ahead.

Firms need an overall strategy or game plan, and they need management structures and systems to enable the plan to be implemented. They need the right people in management positions and they need leadership.

If only half of what was predicted in the previous chapter happens there will have been huge change within the profession. If it all happens, the change will have been seismic.

Stephen Mayson, in his inaugural address as Professor of Strategy and Director of the Legal Services Policy Institute at the College of Law,[1] predicted extensive consolidation of firms and suggested that 3,000 firms might be at risk – one-third of the total for England and Wales. He pointed to the consolidation that has already taken place amongst larger firms – the number of firms with more than 10 partners fell by 30% in the five years to 2006 – and these 366 firms (just 4% of the total) now account for more than half the solicitors in private practice. By contrast, the 'retail' market had seen little consolidation.

The problem for many firms is that they still do not have a real plan, and many of their partners would struggle to know how to prepare one. There is often a wariness or fear of addressing difficult or potentially sensitive issues.

A way needs to be found for firms to develop a real strategy – a robust plan for their future.

The problem areas

There are several problem areas, and they are especially apparent in smaller firms. These would include:

- **A lack of objectivity.** It is often difficult objectively to assess your own firm, especially if you have been a partner for many years – you are too close to it and may find it very hard to view it objectively. This is compounded by the fact that a surprising number of partners have never actually worked anywhere else – they have nothing to compare to.

- **Difficulty in predicting the future.** This is largely because of factors outside the control of the firm – the result has all too often been that the partners have not even tried.
- **Scepticism.** Most partnerships have at least one 'doubter' who will question the value of forward planning, and their influence can be corrosive.
- **Deference**, especially for more senior partners whom younger partners may have been articled to. The relationship can easily be a parent/child type relationship, rather than one of equals.
- **A reluctance to offend or upset** fellow partners by raising difficult or sensitive issues.
- **A lack of time.** In smaller firms especially, the partners invariably see themselves primarily as fee earners. Many came into the law to practise the law and that is what they still enjoy. This can result in a lack of time – and perhaps more importantly, a lack of priority – for anything other than client work.

Doing it well

Some firms have solved these problems and have little difficulty in planning the development of their business. To get it right isn't necessarily that difficult.

Use an external facilitator

A big part of the answer is to change the dynamics of the discussion.

You may meet as partners every month, or perhaps even every week. You may have relatively little to do with each other outside work, or you may meet each other socially. You will know each other, and know each other's foibles, and you are likely to know each other's views – and some of these views may be rather fixed. You may have been round the same discussions many times before. You may never have got beyond the normal stating of positions by each of the partners, and the deadlock that rapidly develops!

In many partnerships it is necessary to break out of these often circuitous discussions and change the dynamics. You may not need a referee as such, but very often the easiest way to change the dynamics of the discussion within a partnership is to involve an outsider. Input from an objective, independent, external facilitator is often the single most important factor that can make the difference between a plan that is mundane and one that achieves something.

Such a facilitator can be someone from within the firm. I have seen firms with, for example, very good HR or marketing directors, who have the respect and confidence of the partners, who have run very successful away days and have helped produce good business strategies. Very often, however, it can be difficult for someone employed by a firm to take the sometimes delicate position between differing groups of partners, without upsetting at least some, if not all, of them! Sometimes someone needs to be able to speak fairly openly to the partners, perhaps saying things the partners would rather not hear. Someone from outside can say what needs to be said and leave – they do not have to worry about offending their employers, and they cannot be fired.

The role is very often that of mediator, an 'uncle' or 'aunt' type figure, whom the partners can talk openly to. One partner commented:

> I have said things to you I have never said to my partners. You have been able to look at us objectively, see us differently to how we see ourselves.

A consultant is well placed to articulate the views in particular of more junior partners, and also those of staff.

I am also aware of firms who have benefited from appointing, often on a part-time basis, a non-executive advisor, sometimes someone who has previously been a managing partner in another firm. Someone who may be in the latter stages of their career, has a pension in place, and who can also speak freely, without too much fear of being fired! They often have the benefit of having experienced similar issues in their own firm.

Involve your key people

The partners may own the firm but they do not have a monopoly on ideas. Increasingly the key people in firms will also include people who will not be partners, who may not even be solicitors – but they will all have ideas to contribute.

These people could be other members of the management team – marketing, finance and HR professionals, or non-partner team leaders. They will have ideas and some of the more successful firms have been better at creating opportunities for them to contribute. These people would, for example, attend partner away days and contribute fully.

You should try fully to engage these people in the process and draw on their ideas. There may be some aspects of the strategy that are confidential to the partners – for example, possible partner retirements or appointments – but apart from these areas, these people should be fully involved in developing the business plan and should attend all the planning meetings.

Involve your staff

Another good way of changing the dynamics is to involve your staff in the development of a forward strategy – at least in the early stages.

Your success as a firm will be a function of many factors, but they will include the degree to which you succeed in making the most of the skills and strengths of your people – your partners but also your other lawyers and support staff. They may not be partners, they may not even be solicitors, but they will have views on the firm and how it could do better. The more successful firms are often those that are able to listen to people at all levels and to learn from them. Very often support staff know exactly what is wrong with a firm and what could be done to make it better. All too often no one has asked them.

When I am asked to help a firm develop a new management structure or a forward strategy I often start by asking everyone in the firm to complete a short questionnaire (a template is included on the attached disk). This example is from one of my clients, a firm in Scotland, and I have included a selection of the replies from their staff:

1. What are the best things about the firm?

It is a happy firm. Some of the partners are helpful and approachable. Nobody breathes down your neck.

Excellent facilities. Good, friendly rapport between members of staff. Access to personal development and training. Opportunities to socialise.

Friendly, relaxed, good supply of biscuits, everyone gets on generally.

Working environment. Good support staff.

The people and the relaxed atmosphere.

Good lawyers. All fee earners working well together. Desire to do well for the client. Modern up-to-date offices with excellent equipment.

2. What would you say the 'values' (the enduring principles that are viewed as important by partners and staff) of the firm are?

The welfare of the staff. The provision of services to clients.

Productivity. Providing the best legal service possible to clients. Making sure staff are happy and productive.

Efficient and value for money service.

Efficiency. Long-term commitment. Knowledge of area.

Fairness and understanding.

Integrity, hard work, sincerity and desire to achieve success.

3. What is it not so good at?

Insufficient support from some of the partners, especially when dealing with specific issues like client complaints or a particular area of work.

Having regular departmental meetings so problem files can be highlighted and assistance provided. It is sometimes difficult to get helpful advice and guidance from more senior members of staff in areas where I lack experience.

Day-to-day communication between partners and staff poor at times.

Praising itself.

The secretaries: always moaning and complaining even when there is nothing to complain about. The partners bend over backwards to care for the secretaries but are never appreciated.

Treating all staff equally – if your face fits you get better treated.

4. If there were three things about the firm you could change what would they be?

Apply a uniform standard in correspondence that goes out of this firm. Presently, there is no corporate identity. Every letter that goes out of this firm is different, depending on the secretary that typed it. Give more support/help when asked.

Not sure. Changes to the way assistance is provided.

Greater role in decision-making. Other people not being so 'jobsworth'.

Nothing.

At the moment there is a fee earner/partner and secretary divide. The firm needs greater teamwork: the secretaries are not interested when team-building events are organised, so compulsory teamwork events could work. Communication: I cannot remember when the last meeting we had was. Management course for the partners: they are only trained as solicitors.

5. How would you assess the way the firm is managed?

Good in some aspects.

I think the firm is managed well. At times there is a lack of communication between the partners and the firm on a day-to-day basis. There is no involve-ment between the partners and staff over such things as marketing, plans for the firm etc.

Sensitively/fairly.

The firm is run and managed by the secretaries. The partners need to remember that they are the managers. The secretaries are paid to work for the partners and not the other way around. A lot of time may be wasted by the partners by them thinking of ways to please the secretaries. We need to be run as a business.

Ok in the circumstances.

6. Which of these apply to the firm?

	Strongly agree	Agree	Disagree	Strongly disagree	Don't know
This is a happy firm	IIII	IIIIIIIIII	III	I	III
The partners work well together	III	IIIIIIIII	III	I	IIIIIIIII
There is a clear plan for the firm's development		IIIIIIIII	III		IIIIIIIIIII
I understand the plan, and my part in its implementation		III	IIIIIIII	I	IIIIIIIIII
Communications are good between partners and staff	I	IIIIIIII	IIIIIIIIIII	II	
Communications are good between departments	II	IIIIIIIII	IIIIIIIIII	I	I
Fee earners are highly motivated	III	IIIIIIIIIII	II	I	IIIII
Support staff are highly motivated	I	IIIII	IIIIIIIIIIII	III	II
The firm is well managed	I	IIIIIIIIIIIIIII	IIII	I	I
My skills are utilised to the full	I	IIIIIIIII	IIIIIIIII	II	I
The firm is good at training and developing people	I	IIIII	IIIIIIIIII	II	III
We have a good appraisal system – that works well		IIIII	IIIIIIIIIII	I	IIII
The firm is good at marketing		IIIIIIIII	III	I	IIIIIIII
We are good at cross selling	I	II	IIIII	I	IIIIIIIIIIII
Our clients receive a good service	IIIIII	IIIIIIIIIIIIII		I	I
We are good at responding to enquiries from prospective clients	IIIIIIIII	IIIIIIIIII		I	II

We have a good reputation	IIIIIIIII	IIIIIIIIIII	I		I
Good use is made of IT	IIII	IIIIIIIIIIIIIIII	I	II	I
File management is good.	II	IIIIIIIIIII	IIII	II	III

This type of questionnaire is an effective way of obtaining people's input and picking up ideas. In the example, this firm was poor at business planning, communications and marketing, but was perceived by staff (a view backed up by clients) as giving a very high level of client service.

Involving staff by means of an initial questionnaire can also help explain to them what is happening, because people can feel nervous at the arrival of someone from outside the firm. It is best for the questionnaires to be returned to someone external to the firm, although, as indicated earlier, I have seen instances where the firms were fortunate to employ excellent directors of HR and marketing, and the questionnaires were returned to them. The key is for everyone to feel they can be open.

Ask your clients and professional contacts

As well as asking staff, it is possible to learn a considerable amount from clients and professional contacts. The latter can sometimes be of greater value than clients as they are often better able to compare your firm with other solicitors.

> You cannot assume that you know whether your client is happy with your service; failing to ask may be interpreted as complacency towards the client. Nor is it remotely unprofessional to ask a client whether your service could be improved in any way.[2]

These comments are from a telephone survey of professional contacts for a small firm in Ireland with one main partner:

> **How would you describe the firm? Could you summarise the firm in one sentence?**
>
> Top class guy. Tells you what you don't want to know. Very good solicitor. Very, very professional and very friendly. Phones you back (some don't phone you back). Takes a personal interest in the clients.
>
> All excellent. Always return calls – some solicitors you have to phone three or four times and they still don't get back to you. Always on top of things.
>
> Progressive, growing, tenacious.
>
> Go ahead in a difficult industry. More focused on solving problems rather than acting superior and throwing up problems – which is what some other firms do. Far happier dealing with him than with most other firms. We give

them most of our work. We give three names, but in reality he is our normal recommendation.

Would always recommend him if client had no solicitor. They are on the ball. Provide very good, professional service. Reasonable sized practice. Don't hang around. Don't let moss grow under their feet like some firms. Will move straight away.

These comments were from commercial clients of a firm in eastern England:

If you can think of one thing that would most improve our service, what would that be?

Fewer holidays.

As everyone would say, putting us at the top of your priority list!

Sometimes a response take a little while. We consider your service is good but, since you want to know the area that would most improve your service would be speed of response.

Updates on changes in the employment law (I think you do already?) – but what about commercial and financial updates?

A broader range of services appropriate to the financial services industry.

A clear indication of what all costs are likely to be, even if it is an estimate based on experience and on the invoice add hours worked and at what rate per hour for each phase of the work.

Supply approximate cost before work is started.

Let me know prices sooner.

At 90% above our director charge-out rates, we find your rates excessive.

Reduce cost of activities.

Ease of parking at your offices.

Develop the plan in stages

Developing an overall business strategy involves a number of stages:

1. The first stage is to establish an overall understanding of the firm today – where you are starting from – by:

- obtaining input from staff, clients and professional contacts – as described above;
- assessing the firm's financial performance – for example, against published benchmarks.

2. Stage two is to obtain the agreement of the partners regarding the overall direction of the firm – what are you aiming for?
3. Stage three is to develop business and marketing plans for each team or department in the context of this overall strategy, that consider what might happen in each of the firm's markets over the coming three to five years.
4. Stage four comprises an action plan, ideally on a quarterly basis, and financial projection.

These stages are discussed in more detail in Chapter 3. A possible structure for a business plan and also a departmental business plan are included on the attached disk.

SUMMARY

- Because of the potential amount of change confronting the profession, firms need to develop a robust business strategy.
- The most effective way of developing a robust plan is to use an external facilitator.
- Involve your key staff in this process.
- Obtain input from all staff in the early stages.
- Obtain input from clients and professional contacts – a view from outside the firm also.
- Develop the strategy in stages.

Notes

1   *Legal Services Reforms: Catalyst, cataclysm or catastrophe?* College of Law, March 2007.
2   Heather Stewart, *Excellent Client Service*, Law Society Publishing 2003.

Paul Stothard, chief executive – Shoosmiths, Basingstoke, Birmingham, Milton Keynes, Northampton, Nottingham, Reading, Solent

How long have you been chief executive for?	I have been chief executive for five years.
How would you describe your firm (top 100, high street, publicly funded etc. . .)?	A top 30 national practice.
How many partners and lawyers does your firm have?	We have 109 salary and equity partners and 230 associates and assistant solicitors.
What is your background? Are you a lawyer?	I am an accountant, having trained with Ernst & Young. I joined the firm in January 2000 as finance director and was elected chief executive with effect from 1 May 2002.
How did you find your first few months as chief executive?	I had the advantage of having worked with the partners for a couple of years before I took on the chief executive role so it was not too traumatic. The toughest part was on the financials, as everyone seemed to use my first year and the impact of the disposal of part of the business as a reason to reduce targets!
What are the best parts of the job?	Seeing talented people realise their true potential.
What are the hardest parts of the job?	Dealing with people who are living in the past and who put up barriers to protect themselves.
How do you find dealing with lawyers?	Very rewarding.
Any tips for managing them successfully?	Don't try to manage them. Just provide a framework and encouragement.
Any tips on motivating the partners and providing leadership?	Be fair, consistent and show up!
How do you see the role of departmental/team leaders?	Critical and, ideally, full-time leadership roles.

What qualities would you look for in your successor?	That is not for me to say but, ideally, they must live and breathe the values of the firm and love the product (our people).
What advice would you give your successor?	Book a meeting with yourself each week to give time and space for thinking and planning.
Any other thoughts?	You are dealing with highly talented and motivated individuals so the worst thing you can do is put a tight management straightjacket around them. Make it fun!

3

Structure, market positioning and values

The importance of structure

For many firms the next few years from 2007 are going to be difficult because they are starting from a position of weakness. Many are achieving low, or only moderate, profits per partner, face difficulties with partner succession, and do not have an especially distinctive position in the markets they operate in. Many of these firms will also have weak balance sheets, and in particular will have high levels of borrowings and insufficient partner capital – in some cases as a result of their low profits, in other cases due to past over-drawing. Many of these firms will not survive the next five years.

The firms still here in 2012, the winners over the next few years, are likely to be those that:

- have a distinctive position in the market – they are different to their competitors, or at least they are perceived as being different;
- are able to attract good people;
- have effective management and in particular people who provide leadership;
- have developed an appropriate business structure.

The latter is especially important because it can have a huge impact on profitability. For firms outside the top 100, many of the most profitable are not profitable because of the type of work they do, the quality of their clients, or the technical expertise of their lawyers – they are profitable because they have an appropriate business structure, and in particular they have good levels of gearing.[1]

The business structure that is likely to be most successful over the next five years is likely to continue to be one with relatively high levels of gearing, and most firms will need business strategies designed to help them develop such a structure.

These firms will require a different role of partners to the one found today – more managers and supervisors than fee earners in their own right, and excellent IT and risk management systems. There will be exceptions, however this is likely to be the key business structure to have in mind when developing your firm's business strategy.

The actual strategy to be followed will very much depend on the areas of work undertaken.

Areas of work

The work of most firms can be grouped into five broad areas:

(a) traditional private client;
(b) traditional commercial;
(c) publicly funded;
(d) volume;
(e) niche or specialist.

Traditional private client work – based around residential conveyancing, trust, probate and wills, privately funded family and litigation for private clients – is the mainstay of many firms:

- existing clients are very important;
- recommendations are also very important;
- it is often a very personal service;
- clients have traditionally been loyal although now it is often highly price sensitive, especially for residential conveyancing;
- clients are often very local – they live or work close to their solicitor.

Traditional commercial client work is very often based around property work for SME (small and medium-sized enterprise) clients and some more general commercial work, both non-contentious and contentious. For many firms:

- it is based around an existing, sometimes quite small, commercial client base; perhaps one or two very active builders or developers, or retail or manufacturing companies;
- it is closely related to particular partners who are well regarded in their locality;
- it is based around particular areas of expertise that are perceived to differentiate the firm from others;
- there is a very close relationships between the partners of the firm and the shareholders/directors of the client;
- these shareholders and directors are also often important personal clients of the firm.

Publicly funded work, although traditionally undertaken by a majority of firms, is increasingly becoming the preserve of a small number who specialise in, for example, crime. It is characterised by:

- low rates of pay;
- a need for most areas of work to be undertaken in volume;
- future price competition.

Despite the low margins, historically some firms – those with high levels of gearing – have been able to achieve high profits per partner.

Volume work has become increasingly important for a number of firms in the last three or four years to 2007. It is often characterised by:

- short-term contracts;
- low margins;
- high volumes;
- referral agencies being of far greater importance to the firm than the actual client.

Once again, despite the low margins this has the potential to be highly profitable.

Niche or *specialist* firms are those that have developed areas of specialisation that enable them to stand out from the competition as having a particular expertise in a certain area – for example, child care, aviation law or complex estates. These firms tend to be characterised by:

- higher margins;
- small teams or departments;
- one or two key people;
- a greater ability recruiting lawyers;
- clients attracted over a much wider geographical area.

Very broadly, over the coming five years, as new entrants come into the market following the Legal Services Bill, firms will have two main choices:

- to become more 'up-market' or specialist;
- to focus on volume and commoditise their business.

Development options

Traditional private client firms or departments:

- are likely to see volumes fall, especially for residential conveyancing;
- will probably reduce in size, in particular in residential conveyancing;
- may start to employ more junior lawyers, rather than solicitors, in order to compete;
- could move up-market, targeting higher income brackets, offering a more bespoke property service – however, the market is likely to be small, and it may be difficult marketing two standards of service;
- could consider offering estate agency and financial services alongside legal services;
- will see that their USP – their 'unique selling proposition' – will be based around client service;
- could develop a range of related services, such as tax and estate planning and services to the elderly.

Traditional commercial firms or departments:

- will need to develop specialisations and team size in order to compete successfully with larger firms;
- will face ever-greater competition from these larger firms who will increasingly target their clients as competition in their own traditional markets increases;
- will feel a need to differentiate themselves from these larger competitors and offer something different to their clients – probably better value for money, but also client service and the benefits of a locally based team, that knows the client and is able to respond more quickly;
- will need to make their teams larger if they are to survive or they will be squeezed out – their better lawyers will be poached to join larger firms.

Publicly funded firms: In the light of government unwillingness to increase funding for legal aid, firms undertaking crime are likely to have to become:

- larger – dealing with work in greater volumes so enabling it to be done more cost effectively and at an appropriate level;
- better at using IT, as it will be required by the Legal Services Commission who will increasingly require firms to communicate electronically.

The situation for firms undertaking civil and family is more difficult as the volume model is less common. Some areas of family can also be difficult to delegate, such as care work and the financial aspects of a divorce. For many firms volumes of work are also less, and in contrast to crime, and perhaps mental health, such work is also very document intensive and as such requires more secretarial support. Whereas a secretary in a crime firm may support five lawyers, one in a civil or family department is unlikely to support more than two – often just one. Where, however, legally aided family work is done in volume, in well geared teams, the work can be profitable.

Publicly funded firms will also need to be much more willing to stop doing areas of work that are no longer viable – they will not be able to cross-subsidise.

Volume work: Firms will need:

- very flexible structures, with short-term contracts for staff and offices;
- excellent IT systems and ways of working;
- to be very good at team working and supervision;
- to be very good at marketing and networking.

Firms that develop *niche* or *specialised* areas of work will need:

- some very good lawyers with technical skills or interest in particular areas of law or sectors that are ahead of other firms;
- people capable of spotting opportunities;
- people capable of marketing their niche area over a wider geographical area.

The actual development route firms choose will depend on their starting points, but also on their culture and the personalities of their partners. It will also very much depend on the partners' values: what is important to the partners?

Values

In her book, *Accelerated Best Practice*,[2] Fiona Westwood defines values as 'those enduring principles that we hold dear and directly influence our behaviour'. She argues that:

> [O]ne of the best ways to identify our own values is to consider why we left a previous organisation. What was it that finally made us say enough is enough? Was it that we were unhappy about the way people were being treated (values of consideration, respect for others and teamwork)? Or that financial considerations appeared to be paramount (values of job satisfaction or duty to society)? Or that the firm seemed to be completely unaware of the importance of good management (values of security, trust and respect for others)?

You need to start by agreeing as partners, but even better including your lawyers and other staff as well, what actually matters to you as individuals. The results can be illuminating and can help achieve cohesion of purpose amongst a partnership that might feel it is moving apart.

Ian Berry and Simon Tupman[3] highlighted the difficulty firms can encounter when trying to define their values:

> Words like 'Communication', 'Respect', 'Integrity', and 'Excellence' sound impressive and possibly resemble your own firm's values. However, generally they are absolutely meaningless. Indeed, these were the corporate values of Enron, as claimed in its 2000 annual report. Most values statements, writes Patrick Lencioni[4] recently in the Harvard Business Review are 'bland, toothless, or just plain dishonest'. He maintains that unless they are deeply ingrained principles that guide all the organisation's actions, they can create cynical and dispirited employees and undermine managerial credibility. They should be inherent and sacrosanct; they should never be compromised, either for convenience or short-term gain.

> Firms need to have a set of values that are true and transparent and that reflect what the firm stands for. If you believe in delivering value for your customers, then that has to be a value or a guiding principle of the firm. Lip service won't do. If those values are not consistent with those of your employees (and vice versa), then you will never win over their hearts and minds – something that is critical when delivering value to customers. Conversely when they are, you will attract like-minded people who are motivated to work for your firm and support those values rather than people who chose to work with you because it's another job that simply pays the bills and adds to the resumé.

A firm's values will have a big impact on the development options open to it. For example, when working with clients, I often find values of 'excellent client service' and 'caring for our staff' can often feature highly. This can be particularly so amongst reasonably long established firms with a traditionally loyal client base. Such firms are likely to find it much easier to develop a strategy based around traditional private client and commercial. They may find it especially difficult to develop a bulk commoditised operation where the actual client may in reality be less important than the intermediary who has referred the client, and where staff may be employed on three-month contracts.

An important starting point, therefore, is to consider and to agree your values.

What are the partners' individual goals?

Having considered the values of a firm, there is also a need for honesty and openness on the part of the partners on their personal plans and goals. Some questions the partners could ask themselves are:

- What level of income do I need?
- When do I plan to retire?
- Would I like to scale down my hours and work part-time?
- Would I like to start a family?
- What type of work do I see myself doing in five years' time?
- Am I happy being more of a manager or do I actually want to be a lawyer?
- What would I like this firm to look like, say in five years' time?
- What do I bring to the partnership?

When a group of people set up a new firm these are things they will discuss at length, however in established firms they are often rarely talked about.

There can easily be differences between partners according to their age and income requirements. Senior partners with just three or four years to go before retirement may, for example, be reluctant to agree to major investment in new offices or staff. Their profit shares are likely to be reduced by the additional costs and they may well have retired before the expected benefits are seen. Younger partners, by contrast, may be keen to see long-term investment and growth because they see it as essential if the firm is to prosper and provide them with a livelihood for the next 20 years or so before they also retire. There may be a middle group of partners who recognise the firm's need for long-term investment but who have a personal need to maximise short-term profitability and drawings because they have mortgages and school fees to pay.

You need, therefore, to be open about what you actually need from the firm personally. This can be surprisingly difficult, especially for lawyers, who invariably hate revealing their 'position'. Years of training as a lawyer almost seem to fly in the face of the more open approach needed when dealing with your fellow partners! Specifically, individual partners need to be willing to disclose:

- how much capital they are able to invest in the firm;
- what levels of profit they require, how much they are able to leave in as capital, and how much they require to draw each month;
- when they plan to retire;
- whether they have any plans to reduce their hours and work on a part-time basis.

Such a discussion becomes especially important where a number of partners are women and wish to start a family. They need to be able to discuss their hopes and plans in an open way and their partners need to be supportive.

It is especially important to know when partners hope to retire, otherwise succession planning becomes virtually impossible. Often partners dislike even thinking about the issue of retirement, and seem to go to great lengths to avoid serious consideration of their personal retirement plans and their income needs. It is often useful for partners to share with each other the pension provision they are making, as this can confirm whether or not their retirement plans are realistic.

As indicated previously, many firms will need to change their business model over the next five years from 2007, by becoming larger, and in particular by developing better gearing. The latter will in many cases be partially achieved by partner retirements. It is highly likely that in many firms the preparation of a business strategy in the light of the Legal Services Bill will result in an acceleration of partner retirements. The resulting firm is likely to have a better structure and will be more profitable. There is a real need to have a robust discussion on the subject of retirements, as they will be key to many firms achieving the change needed.

What is our collective goal?

Having established personal career plans and hopes you should as a partnership agree a collective goal for your firm. For example, if the majority of the partners are in their late 50s it might be fairly obvious that the firm will not survive them and their business strategy should be to move towards a merger with another firm.

As suggested earlier, for many firms the choice is going to be between moving up-market and more specialist, or going for volume. This decision has enormous implicatons for the size, style and feel of a firm and it is highly likely that firms that seriously explore the issue will find a divergence of views, and this may well be the time for teams to split, as a single model may well not be appropriate for all departments.

Changes in firm size can also cause real problems for individual partners. Someone who was appointed partner in a small firm may feel very out of place or uncomfortable in a larger environment. You have to be clear that you are all comfortable with what you are aiming for.

Target market position

Having considered the individual and collective objectives of the partners, you should move on to consider the firm's overall 'market positioning' – both now and in the future.

Market positioning is a difficult concept, yet it is at the heart of building a successful firm. In essence, it is what you want to be known for, by prospective clients and work providers – in effect, your reputation. It is a relatively easy concept for niche firms, but more difficult for general practices that have no particular speciality – of whom there are many.

As indicated in Chapter 2, an external survey of professional contacts is a very good way of ascertaining how you are currently perceived – and this may well be different to what the partners expect or would like. It is quite common for the perception of people externally to be out of date and not to reflect the actual current position of a firm because there can be a significant time lag between something happening and this being reflected in the firm's reputation in the market. A firm may, for example, develop a capability to undertake commercial work, however it may take some time before people outside the firm – professional contacts – associate the firm with commercial work.

The issue is, what would you like your external reputation to be in, say, three to five years' time?

As indicated above, a firm's development options will vary according to the types of work undertaken. Developing a target market position will involve an objective assessment of your firm relative to the competition now – and in the future following the implementation of the Legal Services Bill. What makes your firm different? Where are you strong? Where are you weak?

It is the features that make your firm different to others that attract clients rather than the features that make you the same. It is your specialism in intellectual property or clinical negligence, or the reputation of a particular partner, or the fact that the firm is conveniently located opposite Marks & Spencer that will attract clients.

Hence the need to be clear as a firm as to what your areas of strength are, and to project a clear message to your market (or markets) so that your professional contacts understand the work you do.

This first stage of agreeing a future market positioning is often the most difficult part of the process of developing a forward strategy. With two recent clients I spent four and six months respectively on this single issue – but once decided, the rest of the business plan was straightforward.

Examples of market positioning include:

To be the leading mental health firm in north London.

In terms of overall 'market positioning' the firm is clearly not the largest firm in the County, but it could aim to be regarded as one of the best:

- by clients, in terms of the high standards of service received;
- by support staff – as being a very good place to work;
- by the lawyers as being professionally satisfying;
- by the partners, as being profitable.

To be recognised as being the leading firm in our locality for general work, but to have one or two areas – and agriculture is the first – where we are recognised over a much larger geographical area as having expertise on a par with some of the larger firms in Norwich or Ipswich.

One reason why this part of the process can be difficult is that it is rather intangible, rather hard to take seriously, especially for partners who find management as a whole a difficult area. However, it is key to the development of strategy, and is also good fun!

Having areed an overall target market positioning you can move on to prepare a more detailed plan.

What should the plan look like?

There is no right or wrong format for a business plan – indeed the most valuable part is arguably the process of discussion and idea generation.

The overall aim should be for the plan to be as short and concise as possible. Different types and sizes of firm will need to consider different issues, however the following headings would provide a good starting point for many firms:

1. **Part one – the market and your firm's profile in it**

    • What is your firm's reputation? How would the firm be described by professional contacts or clients? How does the firm compare to others in your town/city/niche? What is its current 'market positioning'?
    • What areas of law is the firm best at? In which areas is it the same as everyone else? Are there any areas it is poor at?
    • What is the mix of work in terms of areas of law and types of client – based, say, on an analysis of fees for the last three years?
    • Where does each department's work come from? Are there any particular professional contacts you receive a lot of work from?
    • What is likely to happen over the next three to five years in each of the firm's markets? What will these changes mean for the firm?

2. **Part two – the firm**

    • How well is the firm managed (in terms of strategic direction and overall management)?
    • How good is its administration, financial and case management systems, its people management?
    • What are internal communications like?
    • Is good use made of technology? How well are fee earners and staff trained in their use of IT?
    • How profitable is the firm and how does it compare to published financial benchmarks?
    • Do a SWOT analysis: summarise the firm's Strengths and Weaknesses, and the Opportunities and Threats facing it.

3. **Part three – overall goal**

- What are the individual and collective aspirations of the partners?
- Agree a future 'market positioning' for the firm.
- What would an attractive goal be in five years' time? How far should the firm have got towards this in three years? In one year?

4. **Part four – action plan**

- A quarterly action plan for the next year.
- An outline plan for the subsequent two years.
- An IT plan.
- A marketing plan.
- A training plan.
- A budget.

The plan is likely to comprise an overall plan or summary for the firm as a whole, along with individual plans for each team and department.

Team or departmental plans

Team or departmental plans will be largely based on the headings above. Some headings will not be applicable, but many will. There may be additional headings you need to include that are relevant to your firm – for example, a multi-office practice may need to include questions regarding the services to be provided from each office, and communications between the offices.

The overall objective is a realistic assessment of the team's markets and the opportunities and threats facing it. The team should consider its strength and reputation relative to other firms for that work.

You may also try to calculate the total value of the market for the team and its market share. For example, for a client in the Home Counties we estimated the total value of commercial work undertaken by firms in their area to be approximately £4.6 million, with an additional 50–100% being undertaken by London firms, giving a total market of approximately £9 million. We could then work out their market share. For another client several years ago, we calculated the total size of the legal market in Bridlington at £1.5 million, of which approximately £1.2 million was undertaken by local firms and £0.3 million being undertaken by firms in Hull.

The size of a market can be approximately calculated by following some simple steps. First, list all the firms in your area who undertake the work in question – say employment law. Then list the actual lawyers each firm has undertaking that work, their names, their ages and a guess as to their likely fees. Use your own fee earners as a yardstick. If your employment partner bills £150,000 a year and an assistant £100,000, take that as your starting point. Because lawyers often know each other and the work they do, it is often possible to make a reasonable guess of someone else's fees. You will know the good lawyers and the poor ones; you will know the people who are efficient and return letters promptly, and you will know the ones who don't. You will also often know which clients different people act for. You can then calculate the overall size of the market for the work done in your area, make an allowance for work done by firms outside the area, and calculate an approximate market share.

Such exercises clearly involve a high degree of guesswork, however they can help to indicate a firm's strength relative to others.

Team plans need to include input from all the lawyers in a team and should include detailed marketing plans and timetables for areas such as:

- press releases;
- articles;
- entertaining;
- seminars;
- corporate events.

A possible template that you could ask all the lawyers to complete is included on the attached disk.

Try to avoid too many action points for each person to do. It is important to be able to review progress and to be able to tick items off. There is nothing worse than an action plan with dozens of points which are never actioned.

Partner away days

A partner 'away day' can be a good way of helping partners to 'buy into' the plan and to contribute in a meaningful way. They are also a great way simply to allow partners to get to know each other better.

The rules for a successful away day are:

- Choose somewhere relaxing away from the office. Try to avoid the temptation to use the boardroom on a Saturday – it does make a difference to get away. It is generally not a good idea to use a partner's house unless you are a very small firm.
- Don't invite spouses or partners – this is business and you need everyone's attention.
- Try to include an overnight stay if possible – it helps team building.
- Involve all partners – equity and salaried – although you may want part of the meeting just for equity partners.
- Invite the other key people in the firm – your non-partner managers.

- Make it informal – no suits.
- Use an external facilitator.
- Write up the action points immediately.

It can be very useful to invite your other lawyers to at least part of the session. They will also find it useful and it is great for them to meet the partners in a relaxed setting away from the office. You may also learn a great deal about them and will see a different side to their personalities. It is a great way of getting to know people you may one day consider for partnership.

Perhaps the main potential benefit of partner away days is simply that of relaxing and spending time with your fellow partners and getting to know people whom you may otherwise actually have little to do with. It is an opportunity to get to know partners from other departments who may also work in another office. You may meet them each month at the partners' meeting but you may not actually know them. One partner commented:

> I had no idea I had so much in common with him.

Perhaps the most common failure is to expect too much from a partner away day. They are part of the process of moving a firm forward and you should not have unrealistic expectations of what may be achieved.

SUMMARY

- **Structure is key to the profitability of many firms, in particular their gearing. Most firms are likely to need a strategy that improves their gearing.**
- **Be aware of the importance of your firm's values.**
- **There is a need for the partners to be open regarding their personal aspirations.**
- **Agree a target market positioning for your firm.**
- **The key benefit of a business strategy is the discussion and process involved.**

Notes

1   The number of other lawyers (or fee earners) in addition to each equity partner.
2   Fiona Westwood, *Accelerated Best Practice: Implementing Success in Professional Firms*, Palgrave Macmillan, 2004, Chapter 2.
3   'Defining and delivering "value" in professional service firms', Ian Berry and Simon Tupman, Remacue.
4   Patrick Lencioni, 'Make Your Values Mean Something', HBR 1 July 2002.

Jenny Beck, managing partner – TV Edwards, London

How long have you been managing partner for?	Four years.
How many partners and lawyers does your firm have?	Seven partners, 35 lawyers.
How would you describe your firm (top 100, high street, publicly funded etc. . .)?	TV Edwards is a medium-sized firm specialising in crime, family, social welfare and personal injury. The majority of our work is publicly funded.
What percentage of your time is spent on management?	60% of my time is spent on management.
How did you find your first few months as managing partner?	Something of a baptism of fire! That said, I think my predominant feeling was one of excitement about the opportunity to change the firm for the better. I rather naively assumed I could continue to run my large caseload at the same time. I therefore found my first few months extremely busy.
What are the best parts of the job?	For me this is the best job I can possibly imagine. I am passionate about my firm and the work that we do, which is why I want to be in control of its future. I love the variety, the challenges, the people contact, the ability to use vision and enthusiasm to drive the firm forward in what are often very difficult circumstances.
What are the hardest parts of the job?	Maintaining a sense of calm and good morale in spite of hostile variables entirely out of my control (for example, current legal aid cuts).
How do you balance fee earning with management?	Badly, I'm afraid. The nature of my practice, which is complex care, necessitates an ability to respond in an emergency and to dedicate a considerable amount of time to my cases, often at short notice. Effective

	management demands the same. I have now (after four years) accepted the need to reduce my caseload in order to ensure my management of the entire firm is not only effective but proactive. I work very long days.
Any tips on motivating fellow partners and providing leadership?	Lead from the front. Always listen. In my view a good managing partner will always have clear vision and proper control. The danger is the desire to drive this forward irrespective of the views of fellow partners. A slight digression from your grand plan or a slight reduction in speed to accommodate your partners can pay dividends. In short, to try to achieve joint ownership of your vision.
How do you see the role of departmental/team leaders?	This is essential in a firm of any reasonable size to assist with supervision, staff management, morale and motivation.
What qualities would you look for in your successor?	Passion about the firm and our goals. Ability to multitask. Enjoyment of people and skill in their management.
What advice would you give your successor?	Make decisions expeditiously. A bad decision which can be changed is better than no decision at all.
Would you consider a non-lawyer chief executive as your successor?	No. In my experience, to properly win hearts and minds you need to inspire confidence not only in your management but also your legal ability. I do not think this is the same for all practices and am sure that there are many in which a non-lawyer could be a very good manager.
Any other thoughts?	The first year of being a managing partner is really about learning the ropes even if you have had the opportunity of shadowing. It seems to me that once the role is owned the real fun begins.

4

Asking some difficult questions

It has always been important not to avoid difficult issues when developing future strategy, however, in the light of the challenges most firms are going to face over the next few years from 2007, this is a time when these difficult issues have to be faced.

In particular there could well be issues for many firms with regard to:

- areas of work undertaken;
- number and locations of offices;
- number of equity partners;
- profit shares and capital contributions;
- partner roles and work contribution;
- admission of other lawyers or professionals into the equity subsequent to the Legal Services Bill.

Part III suggests that the format of many successful firms today in 2007 – and the same is likely to be true for the winners in five years' time – is:

- high levels of gearing – perhaps around six lawyers in addition to each equity partner;
- fees per equity partner[1] of at least £800,000;
- overheads per lawyer of under £15,000;
- hourly cost per lawyer under £70;
- salaries (including equity partner notional salaries) as a percentage of fees under 50%;
- overheads (including allowance for notional rent where the partners own the firm's offices, and notional interest on partner capital) as a percentage of fees under 30%.

The successful firms of the future are likely to:

- be financially well managed;
- have relatively few equity partners;
- be larger than the typical firm of 2007.

Team working is likely to be very important, as this will enable efficient working methods, assist in work being undertaken at the correct level, and result in a lower hourly cost per lawyer.

Work types

Key questions have to be:

- What areas of work should the firm undertake in the future, and what types of clients should it target?
- Are there are any areas of work that are unprofitable, and are likely to continue being unprofitable that should be dropped?
- Are there any areas that should be developed, and whether, for example, the firm should move into related fields such as selling property.

Many firms have already ceased undertaking legal aid work, and many more will have stopped by 2012. Firms that continue providing legal aid work will themselves have to take a more commercial view of the work they do. They may wish to continue to provide everything, but the economics of the work may dictate that they cannot continue to do so. Each area of work has to be profitable in its own right without cross-subsidy from other work types.

The areas of work a firm undertakes will flow from the values the partners have and their aspirations for their firm, but it will be fundamental that each area is also viable. Firms will have very little flexibility in cross-subsidising less profitable areas.

Team, office and firm size

Following on from consideration of the areas of work the firm will actually provide, office location and number of offices are likely to be another potentially difficult issue for many firms.

Part III indicates that the most successful firms today have a gearing of around six lawyers – qualified and unqualified – in addition to each equity partner. For many firms this will be the typical size of a team. There will be variation according to different areas of work, however arguably six other lawyers is about the most one person could effectively supervise. A firm with four or five areas of work and six to ten lawyers working in each area, would produce a firm of 30 to 50 lawyers and four equity partners. This is considerably larger than the typical firm in 2007.

In the 1980s the typical format for many firms was a central office and a number of branch offices, and many firms today still have a branch office network. Sometimes they can be very close, within five miles of each other. When the main competitors were other local firms a local office provided competitive advantage. If the competition is the residential conveyancing department of a bank or supermarket, and if the client is dealing with a call centre hundreds of miles away, is a local office still so important? A principal office five miles away might be fine. Additionally, branch offices can:

- often feel 'second class' compared to the principal office. There is often a perception that the main office gets the best IT equipment, the best coffee, is decorated more often, etc.;
- result in inefficient use of staff. A lawyer may be based at a branch in order to ensure it is staffed, or to continue to provide the service there, but they may have been able to contribute more to the firm if they had been in the main office. The tail can easily wag the dog;
- be difficult to staff during holidays or if staff are ill because there are few people based there. They lack critical mass;
- be isolating places, in particular for a young lawyer sent to run a branch;
- be difficult to manage.

Unless the branch office can develop the team structures suggested above, these small offices are likely to find it increasingly difficult to be cost effective.

Branch offices are often highly emotive issues, however the case must be presented very clearly why a small branch office should be retained, and how it fits into the new world following the implementation of the Legal Services Bill.

The 'ideal' structure, therefore, by 2012 is likely to be:

- teams of at least six lawyers;
- single office firms with at least 30 lawyers (assuming four teams);
- any branch offices themselves will be able to support at least 30 lawyers.

Numbers of partners

As discussed earlier, the key to success in the future for many firms will be their structure, in particular their gearing. This will be achieved over time by recruiting non-partner lawyers, but also by retirement of equity partners. There may well be firms that are not profitable today that will be able to develop a more profitable structure by reducing their equity base.

Important issues to consider are:

- the number of equity partners the firm has now, and how many it should have in the future;
- the competencies required of future equity partners;
- the role of an equity partner and performance expected; the issue of under-performance;
- succession, in particular the difficulty in a growing number of instances of convincing good people to become equity partners;
- the difficulty in other situations, especially for rural practices, of retaining solicitors if you do not offer them equity.

The solution in many instances is likely to be acceleration of retirements with existing equity partners, leaving the equity pool but continuing to work on a consultant or salaried basis. In some cases this will be an ideal result. In many cases they will be able to do what they enjoy – practising the law – and will no longer be weighed down by the responsibilities of partnership.

Possible new structures

One of the very interesting aspects of the Legal Services Bill is the possibility of other lawyers, and also of other professionals such as the firm's finance director, joining the partnership.

This will provide a great opportunity for many firms, as some of their best people may well be legal executives or employed barristers, who up until now have not been allowed formally to join the partnership. Additionally, there are a growing number of law firm professionals – finance, HR, marketing – with in-depth understanding of the sector. For them to be able to contribute capital and participate fully in their firm will be a real opportunity.

SUMMARY

- More so than ever before, firms need to face up to potentially difficult questions. The winners in five years' time in 2012 will undoubtedly be the firms that have faced these issues in a business-like way and resolved them successfully.
- If you avoid these issues they are unlikely to go away – they will return next year, or perhaps the year after, and they are likely to have become more difficult to deal with. They rarely become easier.
- It is often by considering some of the more difficult questions that you make progress.

Note

1   Total fees of the firm divided by the number of equity partners.

Chris Finlay, managing partner – Harvey Ingram LLP, Leicester and Birmingham

How long have you been managing partner for?	I have been managing partner of Harvey Ingram LLP (formerly Harvey Ingram Owston) for six years.
How many partners and lawyers does your firm have?	Harvey Ingram LLP has 32 partners and 130 lawyers, of whom 81 (including the partners) are qualified solicitors. The others are legal executives, trainee solicitors and paralegals.
How would you describe your firm (top 100, high street, publicly funded etc. . .)?	Harvey Ingram is a regional, full service practice. In terms of size, it can be found amongst The Lawyer's 'rising 50' just outside the top 100.
What percentage of your time is spent on management?	Almost 100% of my time is now spent on management.
How did you find your first few months as managing partner?	A blur. It may be nothing more than a coincidence, but the expansion of the firm and increase in profitability which have occurred whilst I have been managing partner, did not begin to take place until my second year in office. I suspect that it took at least a year for me to begin to understand what the job entails.
What are the best parts of the job?	The variety and the ability to influence the course of and the success of the firm.
What are the hardest parts of the job?	The variety and the difficulty in persuading excellent lawyers to see the business as a commercial enterprise.
How do you balance fee earning with management?	I don't. To begin with, I was spending 50% of my time fee earning. This allocation has gradually reduced such that for the last two years, I have been doing little or no fee earning work at all. I found that it

was almost impossible to balance the two, and the danger is that one does both jobs equally badly. In addition, there is always the temptation as a lawyer to put the client work first, which for a managing partner will not always be the right thing to do.

I do not discount the possibility of a managing partner also undertaking fee earning work, as long as the management structure and management support within the firm is sufficiently robust.

Any tips on motivating fellow partners and providing leadership?

I suspect that enough has already been written on this subject! I do believe that a managing partner has an advantage over a non-lawyer chief executive in this particular area. I believe that a managing partner is likely to have more credibility with fellow partners, having worked at the coal face and, in theory, having an understanding of the issues, pressures and demands upon a lawyer partner in a firm of solicitors.

How do you see the role of departmental/team leaders?

In a number of firms, the management role would be split between the managing partner and another partner or partners, usually the senior partner. In my firm, this does not take place, which means that the roles of the fee earning departmental heads and the senior management function heads (IT, business development, HR and finance) are absolutely crucial. It would be impossible for the managing partner to work effectively without a strong management team in place.

What qualities would you look for in your successor?

The ability to earn the respect of those who work within the firm, whether as partners or employees, and the ability to make difficult decisions. Otherwise, I do not think that there is such thing as a 'one size fits all' managing partner and much would depend upon the stage of evolution of the firm when the new person took over.

What advice would you give your successor?	Ensure that you have the full support of a strong management team and don't expect or try to be popular!
Would you consider a non-lawyer chief executive as your successor?	Yes.

II

Managing and motivating your people – and leadership, the key ingredient

Leadership, management and managing change

If, over the next few years from 2007, firms are going to increase in size they will need to improve their management. They will also need people who provide leadership.

There are likely to be three aspects of management that will be especially important:

- the managing partner or chief executive;
- team or departmental management;
- professional support managers or directors in areas such as finance, HR, marketing and IT.

These three areas are considered in subsequent chapters in this part. This first chapter considers leadership – as opposed to management and administration – and also touches on the role of equity partners, and how change can actually be achieved.

Leadership, management and administration

> Effective leadership In any law firm is helping it develop and seeking the development of leadership qualities in others.
>
> Michael Shaw, Cobbetts

'Leadership' is very different to 'management' or 'administration'. It can be very useful periodically to review the management of your firm, and assess its management under these three headings, and ask whether the correct people are doing each function.

The day-to-day administration of a firm is a time-consuming, detailed task that partners too often become embroiled in, but that generally they should avoid. Except for in the very smallest of firms, administration should be something that is delegated to support managers, something that partners may supervise, but should not actually do themselves.

In some firms 'management' does not extend beyond day-to-day administration and ensuring the firm functions properly. Some managing partners have said that essentially, when appointed, that was what their partners required of them. They needed someone to oversee cashiers, deal with issues concerning the building, deal with staff issues – basically to ensure a smooth-running ship.

Such styles of management tend to be very *reactive*, as little time is devoted actively to moving the firm forward. The partners invariably spend most of their time fee earning, and partner meetings are often painful affairs. The managing partner is generally expected to spend most of his or her time fee earning. The other partners in such firms invariably still expect to have a say in most aspects of the running of the firm – they see themselves very much as owners, and partner meetings often deal with the minutiae. Little is delegated to the managing partner and the role can be frustrating and demoralising.

Firms with this style of management are likely to be amongst those who will struggle over the next five years because:

- they will not have anticipated the change that is coming;
- they will have not have grown their firm to a size that is sustainable in the long term.

A more *proactive* style of management would be one that:

- develops a future strategy – taking into account the values of the firm, and the partners' individual objectives as described in Part I;
- periodically reviews the firm's operational structure – its offices, departments and teams – in the light of that strategy;
- periodically reviews the management structure needed to achieve the strategy;
- identifies the correct people to take part in management.

As with all successful businesses, the latter point – identifying the correct people to take part in management and to lead the firm – is of fundamental importance. Firms have to play to the strengths of their people and utilise those strengths, be they amongst the partners or other staff. Hopefully some of these people will also demonstrate leadership.

Warren Bennis[1] contrasts 'managers' and 'leaders':

Managers . . .	Leaders . . .
Managers administer	Leaders innovate
Managers maintain	Leaders develop
Managers ask how & when	Leaders ask what & why
Managers focus on systems & procedures	Leaders focus on people
Managers rely on control	Leaders inspire trust
Managers take a short term perspective	Leaders have a longer term perspective
Managers accept the status quo	Leaders challenge the status quo
Managers do things right	Leaders do the right things

As firms increase in size, they will do so because they have at least some people who are leaders.

Operational and management structure

When reviewing the management of your firm, a good place to start is its structure – in terms of both its operation, and its management.

Operational structure

Operational structures are important because if you get them wrong the business itself can be harmed.

'Operational structure' refers to the structure of the firm in terms of its offices, departments and teams. Questions to consider will include:

- Should the firm be single-office or multi-site?
- Should departments be managed on an office or cross-office basis?
- Should the firm operate according to legal disciplines (conveyancing, litigation, etc.) or types of client (private client, business clients)?
- Can departments be subdivided into more specialised teams?

Traditionally many high street firms have been organised on an office basis, and in particular have produced accounts on an office basis. They have often suffered as a result because this focus on the office rather than the firm can influence behaviour. Firms that may actually have been large in their region have operated in the same way as smaller local competitors because their lawyers did not look beyond their own office. They would rarely refer clients to more specialised colleagues in other offices as that would have affected the fees of their office. This happens especially where the lawyers are in part remunerated on the basis of the fees of the office, or their own fees.

The task for management is periodically to review and challenge the current operational structure and consider how it needs to evolve.

Management structure

Having agreed on an appropriate operational structure you need to design a management structure actually to manage the firm.

Over the years there have been a range of management styles from the once highly successful all-powerful senior partner or benevolent dictator to today's full-time managing partners and chief executives. Between the two is a wide range of different styles, but increasingly:

- partners are recognising that in all but the smallest of firms, it is better for day-to-day management to be delegated to a small management team – quite possibly including non-lawyers;
- there is one person in overall charge – a managing partner or chief executive;
- firms are starting to recognise that management does not have to be exclusively the preserve of partners, but that other people may have a role to play.

The actual structure will vary from firm to firm, but the underlying principle should be one that:

- allows effective line management to take place;
- is responsive to the markets the firm operates in.

Having agreed the structure it is important to ensure that the correct people are identified to take up management roles. Traditionally partners have been responsible for managing a department, however this assumes they are the correct people to do so. In very small firms there is logic in the owners of the business taking responsibility – it is their money at risk. As firms grow, it is still the capital of the equity partners that is at risk, however there comes a point where they need to consider whether they are still the correct people actually to manage the firm. Do they have the right skills? Is it the best use of their time?

The role of equity partner

In most firms the equity partners still see their main role as fee earning – indeed in many, especially those with low levels of gearing, the partners will be the main fee earners. They will spend 95% of their time on their own client work, with just part of their time spent supervising their team or on marketing. They may not have much of a team – there may only be one or two other fee earners working with them, and these fee earners may in reality be working on their own, hence they may not be working as a real team. The partner may be too busy to take on extra work so will see little benefit in marketing. The partner entered the law to practise the law, and is quite happy with this role – it is what he or she enjoys.

Firms that have too many of this type of partner will be amongst those that struggle over the next few years from 2007. You need your partners to be more than just fee earners. They need to evolve.

> It is not the strongest of the species that survives nor the most intelligent, it is the one that is most adaptable to change.
>
> Charles Darwin

The equity partners in the firms that prosper over the coming years are likely to see their job differently – in particular, they will view their main role as that of a 'business builder',[2] someone who adds value to the firm and creates growth. Technical lawyers can be employed actually to do the work. The really important skill, and one that is generally in limited supply, is people who can develop and grow the business.

These people, and they do not have to be partners, will increasingly see their role as:

- spotting opportunities – for cross-selling internally, and seeing opportunities externally;
- building teams to exploit these opportunities;
- supervising their team – or employing technically competent lawyers to supervise;
- developing members of their team;
- ensuring the team and the firm is profitable and cash rich.

These people will also often display leadership and will be good at motivating staff.

Motivating staff

As firms evolve and develop it will be ever more important for their partners and managers to find ways of motivating the people who work in them.

In 2007, Law Society research into staff retention[3] identified a number of key factors in achieving a well-motivated work force:

- a good supervisor or manager;
- good opportunities for career progression / transparent career path;
- challenging and interesting work;

- competitive salary and benefit package;
- good working environment / colleagues.

The survey found that:

> professional staff will be most motivated to stay at a firm if they feel challenged in their work and are able to take on a good level of responsibility within that work. Professional staff thrive on the social dimension of working in a good team and having contact with their clients. Where supervision occurs it has the most power to motivate staff to stay where it is seen to help them develop in their role.

Research amongst a small number of junior solicitors and support staff for the first edition of this book identified very similar motivating factors:

- For a young secretary:
  - good working conditions;
  - job security;
  - appreciation for work completed;
  - interesting work;
  - feeling of being involved;
  - high salary.
- For a young assistant solicitor:
  - interesting work;
  - high salary;
  - promotion within the firm;
  - good working conditions;
  - feeling of being involved.

Many firms are poor at motivating their staff, and part of the problem is that they do not have a real understanding of the factors that make for a well-motivated environment. Fee earners in particular are often assumed to be primarily motivated by money, but as the research indicates, this is only one of the factors. The 'soft' factors that often cost little are frequently overlooked.

In order to retain your best people, you need to pay fair salaries and offer a good overall package. It also means:

- **Showing appreciation for work completed.** In particular encouraging your partners and other fee earners to say 'thank you' more often – something many lawyers, especially when under pressure, are poor at. It costs the firm nothing yet can do wonders for motivation!
- **Helping people to feel involved by sharing information** – especially financial – and involving them in team or firm-wide meetings.

- **Thinking more carefully about who actually does what with a view to giving more people work that is interesting.** Whilst all firms will have much work that is relatively boring and repetitive, there is always some that is interesting, especially for more junior people and for support staff. If you are able to give more people some tasks that they enjoy and consider important, they will feel more motivated and will give the firm more in return.
- **Being willing to discuss promotion prospects in an open way.** As discussed earlier, the key to profitability in many firms will increasingly be the number of equity partners relative to other fee earners and the result will be that many solicitors who might have expected equity will not get it. They may, however, become salaried partners and you may be able to offer them an overall package and feeling of self-respect that means they stay with your firm. But it has to be discussed, and it has to be reasonably transparent.
- **Providing your staff, especially your support staff, with good working conditions.** This may mean reasonably new furniture, a reliable computer, flexible working or air-conditioned offices. In many cases the starting point is to ask them.
- **Making it very clear that fee earning is not the only thing that is valued** – i.e. team enhancement, good use of IT, good relations with fellow staff and clients, and ultimately a contribution to management, are all very important.

Respect

Allied to motivation is the concept of 'respect', and this is itself related to a firm's values. Not just respect for the senior partner, but for the contribution all staff can make to a firm's success.

Traditionally many partners have been poor at showing respect and sometimes even courtesy towards their staff (and their fellow partners) – and some still are. Once again, there is a real difference in the 'feel' of firms where the partners have addressed the issue, and in the long term firms that have addressed this are likely to be more successful.

The key to this is the recognition that each firm member plays a valuable role, and not simply as a fee generator or income earner. In assessing each person, proper weight has to be given to management issues and other forms of contribution to the success of the firm. If, on honest assessment, an individual is found not to be contributing in a global sense, then this should be addressed in the person's appraisal interview or it should be recognised that they do not have a long-term future with the firm. The key to the assessment, however, is a recognition that a good contribution to the management of the firm, or areas other than straight fee earning, count as valued 'work'.

Some firms have agreed a partner/staff protocol that all partners have signed. These can be useful tools in making it more difficult for partners to obstruct management. They might include an agreement to:

- respect each other;
- share responsibility;
- criticise ideas not people;
- keep an open mind;
- attend all meetings;
- listen constructively;
- keep promises.

Sometimes the protocol is in the form of a small statement that is put on notice boards and distributed to all staff – once again making it more difficult for partners to start going back on the principles.

Getting people to change

Most people dislike change and find it difficult to deal with, especially if they are faced with change on too many fronts. It is easy for change to be intimidating and it also requires the one thing most fee earners lack – time.

People in the early part of their careers normally don't have major problems with adjusting to change. They may object vehemently to changes that affect their day-to-day life, such as a new secretary, or new office, but they are normally able to adjust to change much easier than colleagues in their 50s and 60s – although there are some notable exceptions. Some firms have senior partners who put their younger colleagues to shame with their willingness to embrace new technology and change in general.

There are two main groups of people who are often resistant to change:

- some (but not all) more senior partners, especially those with heavy workloads, who can be reluctant to adopt new working methods;
- some (but once again not all) more senior secretaries (often those who work with the partners who are resistant to change). They have often been with the firm for years, are only really there for the salary and have a very 'nine to five' attitude. These people can be a particular obstacle, and it is remarkable the impact just one or two such people can have.

These two groups of people can be a considerable barrier to change and can cause endless frustration to other partners and members of staff.

There are perhaps four main areas that people have always had difficulty with that are likely to become even more of a problem:

1. **Changes in workflows due to the Legal Services Bill**

    Many firms are likely to see work levels falling in certain areas due to the Legal Services Bill. We have already seen the change that occurred in both defendant and claimant insurance work in recent years. Many firms that used to do defendant work have suffered marked falls in work levels as insurance companies have cut their panels, and many that undertook claimant work have seen traditional sources of personal injury work dry up over a period of time and go instead to 'claims farms'. The traditional workflows have changed. Clients who would previously have simply used a local solicitor are being channelled elsewhere.

    It is quite likely we will see similar change taking place over the next few years in areas such as residential conveyancing and other traditional high street areas of work.

2. **Difficulty adapting to changed working methods**

    Most people are now good at using technology – they use it as part of their daily work and use e-mail and the internet constantly. Where they have greater difficulty is in 're-engineering' their work and understanding how a service they view as bespoke might be provided by a competitor in a commoditised way, and therefore at a lower cost.

3. **An apparent reluctance to change because of high caseloads taken on in order to maintain personal fee levels**

    Many fee earners – especially partners – can appear unenthusiastic to change, whereas the real problem lies in their workloads In many firms there is competition amongst partners to achieve high personal fees, and this is especially so in those firms that place too much emphasis on individual fee targets. In some cases this is imposed from above, in others it comes from below, as fee earners often have a natural desire to compete with each other. The result can be fee earners with extremely high caseloads.

    The last thing someone struggling with a very high caseload needs is additional jobs or apparently unnecessary changes to their work.

4. **An apparent reluctance to change and to perform caused by a slowing up with age – and appearing stubborn as a result to younger colleagues**

    Some partners are able to work and bill at the same levels when in their 50s and 60s as they did in their 30s and 40s – but most cannot.

More senior partners in firms also invariably spend more of their time on the management of their firm. Many firms still set individual fee targets and do not make allowance for these factors, instead giving all partners the same targets. The result can be that these more senior partners feel under immense pressure to achieve the same levels of fees as their colleagues 20 years younger. Because they are more senior and often dealing with more complex cases, they often believe they should achieve high fee levels and are surprised when they struggle. The result can be that they work ever longer hours and start hanging on to work they should delegate.

A by-product of the difficulty in managing change is that the management burden often falls on just a few people – sometimes some of the highest billing partners. They know that if they don't try to manage the firm no one else will. These people embrace change but because they are already very busy they finish up with an even greater workload as they try to combine fee earning with management.

A common theme underlying all of these issues is that partners and fee earners are increasingly struggling to cope with growing volumes of cases without changing their working methods.

The result is fee earners who have very little time for anything other than fee earning who, over time, can become demoralised. The answer to increased pressure on fees is often seen to be to take on more cases and work longer hours. A better solution might be to be more selective in the work taken on, to put more thought into the level of fee earner who should actually do it, and to think more seriously about whether fee earners can be smarter in their working methods.

In many cases a big part of the solution is to move away from the traditional lawyer/secretary structure and move towards better team working. By working together as a small unit, and provided everyone is properly supervised, the lawyers are able to deal with a higher volume of cases much more efficiently. It can help make the job of being a lawyer more enjoyable.

This concept of a fee-earning unit – a qualified lawyer, paralegal and secretary – is even more important when the lawyer has a significant management role. Such support is particularly important in small firms, where the partner often takes on a management workload in addition to a full caseload – an untenable long-term situation.

So, in helping people to change, a good starting point is to try to understand better the work and working methods of individual fee earners, the problems they face, and the things they enjoy. You also need to consider how you actually want people to use their time.

Time management

Partners in many firms will typically work 10-hour days, sometimes more, rarely less. This means that most partners spend perhaps 2,300 hours a year in the office – they arrive in the office by, say, 9 am and leave by 7 pm; and they work five days a week for 46 weeks a year (six weeks allowed for holidays, illness, etc.).

At present the only target most firms set relates to chargeable hours, and a figure of 1,100 hours a year is often regarded as a good goal. Many larger firms would expect their lawyers to work very much more than this, and indeed a 2003 survey of legal aid firms[4] found the average for small legal aid firms to be around 1,300 hours a year.

Few firms set targets for anything other than chargeable time, and of course this sends out a message to everyone that only chargeable time is valued. A minority, and these will be amongst the firms that are more successful over the coming years, will also set targets for:

- supervision;
- marketing and business development;
- personal training and research;
- administration – housekeeping.

The starting point is to define what you actually want your partners to do – what is their role? In particular, how should individual partners spend their time? What is each good at? What are their strengths?

You should ask the same questions of everyone else. If you have a junior partner who is excellent at marketing and networking, why give that person a high fee-earning target, which means he has little time for marketing? Try to identify the real contribution each person can make to the firm.

SUMMARY
- **Distinguish between administration, management and leadership.**
- **Periodically review your operational and management structure – make sure you have the right people in leadership roles.**
- **Utilise the management skills and abilities of all your staff – not just the partners.**
- **Re-appraise the role of your equity partners.**
- **Aim to create a motivated work force.**

Notes

1   Warren Bennis is an American scholar, organisational consultant and author who is widely regarded as a pioneer of the contemporary field of leadership studies.

2   Professor Stephen Mayson, Managing Partner Forum, Manchester, April 2007.

3   *The great 'quality of life debate' – Best practice in staff retention and job satisfaction,* Law Society 2007.

4   Otterburn *Legal Consulting: Department for Constitutional Affairs – Review of Demand, Supply and Purchasing Arrangements – Survey of Legal Aid Firms,* 2003.

Philip George, managing partner – Birkett Long, Chelmsford and Colchester

How long have you been managing partner for?	Five years.
How many partners and lawyers does your firm have?	18 partners and about 35 other lawyers.
How would you describe your firm (top 100, high street, publicly funded etc. . .)?	Aspiring regional.
What percentage of your time is spent on management?	75%
How did you find your first few months as managing partner?	Easier than expected (but then I did have the benefit of 12 months shadowing the then managing partner).
What are the best parts of the job?	Being at the helm of a successful and growing business, and seeing it develop. I take particular pleasure in being a small part of the career progress of our bright young lawyers.
What are the hardest parts of the job?	1. The first day of any new financial year.
	2. Dealing with difficult people – happily we don't have many of them, but the partnership structure can be cumbersome when dealing with uncooperative individuals.
How do you balance fee earning with management?	By working long hours and having well-developed time-management skills!
Any tips on motivating fellow partners and providing leadership?	Always allow other people to think that the best ideas are theirs even when they are actually yours!
How do you see the role of departmental/team leaders?	Absolutely crucial. In anything other than the smallest firms each team is a mini-business in its own right with

	the team leader as its managing director. My key relationships are with the heads of department, who filter my ideas down through the firm via their teams (and in turn filter their team's ideas up to me).
What qualities would you look for in your successor?	You haven't left enough space for me to answer! Seriously though, I think the most important qualities are good organisational and listening skills, and the ability to take decisive and difficult decisions even when these are unpopular. A thick skin helps!
What advice would you give your successor?	Make sure that you have good people in all the key positions so that you can delegate effectively and ensure that you have time to deal with policy issues and matters that genuinely need *your* attention.
Would you consider a non-lawyer chief executive as your successor?	No – but only because we have suitable partners willing and able to do the job. I think that we are likely to be led by a non-lawyer one day.

6

The key person – the managing partner

The job of managing partner will vary considerably from firm to firm, in particular according to its size and structure. However, as discussed in Chapter 5, any successful organisation, regardless of sector or size, needs someone who provides leadership. It is one of the key ingredients for success today, and will become ever more important for firms in the future.

The winners in the future will be those firms who identify someone with the skills to do the job successfully and who give this person the time to do it.

What does the job comprise?

The role will vary, but here are some thoughts from a group of managing partners,[1] drawn from mainly larger provincial firms:

Job is to challenge the status quo, unsettle fellow partners and get them thinking. Have to show a lead and get buy in.

Another important job is spotting opportunities and making them work.

Role?
- Plan every three years on a strategic basis. There is going to be a challenge every three years. Here are the challenges facing us; here is where the best performing firms could be in three years' time. In order to succeed we are going to have to position ourselves here. . . How are we going to respond?
- Need to challenge what is already a reasonably successful business in order to get a higher level in a short period.
- In a dynamic market it is incumbent on the role to challenge. Need a big picture then action plans for each team.
- Need to have a range of personal and business skills that most do not display.
- To manage people's insecurities – but not to have any yourself.
- To give direction.
- To lead by example.

- To police the culture.
- To convey importance of management skills to department heads – to demonstrate that a person's contribution can be other than fee earning.

Part of the role is spotting and developing talent:

- People who are good stand out in their departments.
- Give people opportunities to excel in areas other than fee earning. Can be difficult in larger firms where fee earners are viewed primarily as a resource for generating fees.
- If you have someone with a special talent let the managing partner have direct access. People who are good business developers are more valuable than good lawyers.

It is important at the outset actually to agree what the job entails, what authority levels you have, and how much time you will be given to do it. Historically, many (in particular in smaller firms) have seen the job as primarily to do with administration and the smooth running of the firm. As discussed previously, this is something the managing partner might oversee – not do personally. The core of the job should be very different.

Normally a managing partner should expect to do two three-year terms. It is often only at the end of the first term that a managing partner starts to perform effectively. It is during the second term that they start making real headway.

There are few people who can spend more than six years leading an organisation, however in recent years, for the first time in the law in the UK, a group of career managing partners has evolved, in much the same way that happened amongst accountants a decade earlier. Some of these people have been managing their firms highly successfully for 10 or 12 years, more in some cases, and they still have much to give. They are exceptional people.

It is also important to give them the time to manage. All too often, especially in smaller firms, managing partners are expected to combine management with a near full caseload. In many instances the managing partner is also the firm's highest fee earner. Increasingly, firms will need to take a view as to how the skills and abilities of their key people can be best used. A partner may well be capable of earning a reasonable level of fees – perhaps £150,000 to £250,000 a year – but would actually be of far greater value 'actively managing' the firm and its lawyers.

A job outline for a managing partner in a smaller firm might be along the lines of:

1. Responsible for:

   (a) overall management of the firm;
   (b) day-to-day administration, including finance and accounts;
   (c) overall achievement of the firm's business plan.

2. Department heads report to managing partner, together with accounts manager. Managing partner accountable to partnership.
3. Finance:

   - Oversees preparation of budget annually.
   - Reviews monthly management accounts and cashflow.
   - Monitors monthly performance of fee earners – fees and hours.
   - Reviews quarterly report of departmental profitability with partners.

The support directors of a mid-sized provincial firm prepared this job outline for their managing partner:

1. To develop a strategic vision for the firm along with the Management Board. To ensure change management is successful.
2. To be an equal member of the management team which runs the day-to-day business with devolved responsibility from the Management Board.
3. To be a fee earner and maintain legal skills (20–30% time).
4. To understand the business as a whole and thus be able to deal on a personal basis with many of the top-line enquiries from prospective clients.
5. To spend time with other partners.
6. To motivate, communicate, direct, coordinate and enthuse employees and build internal relationships.
7. To be a conduit for business issues within the firm.
8. To oversee compliance issues.
9. To be an ambassador for the firm, build external relationships.
10. To lead by example, internally and externally and set standards.

In order to fulfil the role properly, in even the smallest of firms the managing partner must spend at least a quarter of his or her time on management. In some of the most successful small firms the managing partner may well be full-time, or near full-time, and much of the role will be devoted to business development and marketing.

As firms grow there comes a point where the managing partner should always be full-time, or near full-time – certainly when a firm reaches a size of 30 to 40 lawyers, it should be a near full-time role. That is the format of the successful firms today, and will be even more so in the future.

What qualities do you need?

The first edition of this book included a set of qualities that Michael Shaw, managing partner of Cobbetts, a leading provincial firm, identified as the 10 key qualities a managing partner should have. They are as relevant today as they were in 2002:

- **Arrogance** – you simply have to believe that at least your ideas for the future of the firm are as good as, or better than, those of anybody else. Of course, if you are like me then you will probably suffer from permanent self-doubt (that you can't share) and arrogance should not stop you from listening to (and using) everyone else's ideas;
- **Credibility** – consultants and academics often seem to suggest that it is bizarre that the usual qualification for leadership is the individual's history for achieving very high billings. Of course high billings in themselves don't make a leader but it does provide a basis for credibility. There has been a clear record of commitment and achievement for the firm and the last thing you can ever stand to risk is someone within the firm saying, '. . . but you don't know what it's like at the coal face';
- **Honesty** – unless you possess other superhuman abilities, dishonesty and insincerity are spotted instantly by those within the firm and your clients. This is applicable on an individual basis and also collectively as a firm. We all get things wrong and certainly I have found it actually does some good when you are prepared to tell everybody else that is the case;
- **Respect** – this is not so much respect for you, but the respect you have for everybody else. If that is instilled within the firm, then the recognition of potential on the part of everyone regardless of status is axiomatic. Neither you, your partners, nor your qualified staff has a monopoly on wisdom. Some of our youngest support staff have the most profound understanding of clients' needs and how they should be fulfilled. If you do not recognise the potential of all, you will not bring out the best;
- **Courage (or recklessness – I'm not sure which)** – our training teaches us to abandon creativity and avoid risk taking, but in trying to create a lead you can't follow the herd. Yes, you can learn lessons from others but what is right for your firm is quite different to any other. Accept that some things will work, but not everything;
- **Security** – insecurity has to be abandoned both in your role as leader and also in the roles of others within the firm. Undoubtedly, personal insecurity tends to be the biggest barrier to change and I have found the biggest demand upon my time is talking to colleagues to help them face those hurdles and build their confidence;

- **Open-mindedness** – be prepared to listen to new ideas from whatever source and don't interpret a difference of opinion as being criticism;
- **Communication, communication, communication . . . ad infinitum** – recognise that your firm is populated by bright people who will generally cooperate fully – once they have gained an understanding of what you are trying to do;
- **Friendships** – you need your friends to tell you when you've got it wrong, and your best friends to tell you when it's OK, because nobody else will;
- **Modesty** – yes, take credit while it's going, but don't let the necessary display of self-belief delude you. Above all else, remember that the moment you feel smug, you have failed.

This set of skills is going to limit the number of potential candidates, however it provides an indication of the type of person you should be looking for. Successful managing partners are normally equity partners, as it is very difficult for a salaried partner to have the necessary authority, and they should if possible be part of the 'power base' of the firm.

Do not assume your managing partner is going to be one of the most senior partners in the firm. Be prepared to look further down the partner list, perhaps to someone in his or her late 30s. It is also very useful to have a managing partner who is willing to take risks.

You should always be aware of the issue of succession and should look for a wide range of personal skills in your future partners. Be prepared to embrace ideas such as personality profiling to get a better assessment of prospective partners and senior staff.

Above all, be clear about the role, the level of authority, the term of office, and what the person is expected to do after ceasing to be managing partner.

The more difficult aspects of the role

Managing partners are often faced by two particular areas of difficulty:

- lack of time for those who also have a high fee-earning workload;
- having to deal with issues regarding fellow partners:

One or two difficult people and problems can sometimes outweigh the positive; the economy is not predictable; clients can have unreasonable demands which encourages wheels to fall off.

Fee earners, including team leaders and senior partners who do not perform effectively the administrative and management tasks delegated to them. Lack of real sanctions!

The need sometimes to persuade 20+ people to do something. Partner interference/subversion of plans.

Succession; premises; conflict between management duties and client demands. Getting decisions at partnership level. Getting policies implemented firm-wide. Recruitment. Statutory and similar requirements – employment, money laundering, financial services etc., etc.

Authority to enforce agreed decisions with other partners; partners making decisions without consideration of impact on whole firm; resistance of partners to change/innovation, and to accept that standards imposed on staff should also apply to themselves.

Balancing the time spent as managing partner and professional work; the unrealistic expectation of partners who want to be part of the management of the firm by being involved in day-to-day decisions; the same partners being dilatory in carrying out requests of the managing partner or following laid down procedure; not enough hours in the day.

Ensuring effective communication; dealing with insecurities on the part of partners.

Partners' unwillingness to accept/embrace change; resistance to 'management'; danger of proceeding at pace of the slowest to come on board.

The nature of the partnership structure is unwieldy.

A dysfunctional management team; insufficient time to undertake it properly; a lack of appreciation of management issues on the part of other partners and staff; no qualifications or training in the necessary skills of herding cats.

The areas of difficulty can be summarised as being primarily concerned with:

- fellow partners:
  - partners who are under-performing;
  - partners who do not manage effectively or interfere;
  - lack of sanction;
  - getting agreement from a large number of people;
- getting people to change;
- lack of time.

Some of the comments reflect the limitations of partnership itself as a vehicle, but others reflect the difficulty of managing a business which is evolving and in which the job of managing partner is itself changing. Several of the comments highlight the particular issues of levels of authority and also lack of sanction over fellow partners.

Dealing with fellow partners

Many of the hardest problems a managing partner has to deal with concern fellow partners and are often aggravated by the lack of any real sanction over a fellow partner. It is a particular problem with a partner who is under-performing, or, worse, is being uncooperative.

What makes a person under-perform?
- laziness;
- lack of security;
- being over-promoted;
- the firm and business have changed – the person has not.

Typically they are deviant in non-financial areas – they undermine other areas.

If you let it continue it permeates and people do not believe you in other areas you are trying to tackle.

Does not matter how, but has to be dealt with.

57/58 is the age people can start to have difficulties. People go off the boil at different points. A divorce can affect someone for three years. We have a voluntary fixed share, fixed term scheme at a certain age. They get their capital back so they can invest it.

It is very difficult to change the behaviour of a mature partner. Need to be explicit and take subjectivity out of it.

When you deal with it they are often happier.

Your partnership agreement will have provisions for expulsion of a partner, but these are unlikely to help in the event of a partner who is under-performing or is simply uncooperative. Of course these are two very different situations that are likely to require very different solutions.

Most professionals have phases in their careers where their performance is poor, and in most cases the problem passes and matters improve. Occasionally the problem is more serious and long-term, and is frequently the result of other underlying difficulties, such as:

- long-term changes in the market, resulting in changed patterns and volumes of work – something likely to happen more frequently over the coming years;
- the introduction of new technology or working methods which partners may find difficult to adjust to;

- problems at home, especially marital;
- stress, depression or other forms of illness;[2]
- perceived pressure from younger partners.

Invariably the starting point for dealing with under-performance is a willingness to talk with the partner and to listen to the partner's concerns. The problem may take many months to resolve and may require many sessions with the partner, however provided the person still has a positive attitude towards the firm the effort is invariably worthwhile.

The more difficult area is where partners are simply being unhelpful, difficult and uncooperative. The starting point in dealing with this type of situation is often the strength of the managing partner's own authority within the firm and the level of support for the managing partner amongst the partnership as a whole.

The situation can be complicated if there are divisions within the partners, however if the managing partner has the backing of the partners at least a start can be made in tackling the problem. Once again, the starting point is a discussion with the person concerned with a view to listening to their perspective and trying to negotiate progress. Often, even the most unreasonable person has an element of justification in their cause.

The managing partner will need good 'people skills' in this type of situation, and the approach taken will depend on the culture and size of the firm. The managing partner will need to be able to listen effectively. The general rule, however, is not to 'duck' the problem or avoid it, because it is unlikely to go away, and can easily result in a terrible example to others that will simply serve to undermine management within the firm.

Sometimes it is possible to achieve much via alternative tactics, in particular a general change in management or working methods, such as:

- appraisals and development reviews being extended to include partners in order to provide a forum for a regular discussion about a partner's performance;
- greater openness about financial performance so as to provide 'gentle embarrassment' and a degree of peer pressure, especially if such information is made available to all members within a team;
- monthly marketing reports to be produced by all fee earners and circulated for information to all members of a team, once again to create peer pressure.

If none of this works, the situation generally has to be brought to an end, and a parting agreed with the partner. Obviously the terms of your partnership agreement will be key, so there is much to be said for having one in place well before any problems arise. Very often the partner concerned may need professional support and counselling – and the managing partner will need the support of his or her partners. This type of situation can take many months to resolve and can occupy a huge amount of a managing partner's time.

The first 12 months – learning the ropes

The role of managing partner can be a daunting one to take on, and an important part of a managing partner's job should be to identify and start developing potential successors.

Unless you are extremely lucky, there will generally be relatively few candidates and they need to be nurtured with care. The ideal way for them to develop their own management skills is through a team or departmental management role. Also, as soon as a potential candidate is identified they should start attending appropriate management seminars and forums – anything that will start to develop their management skills.

CASE STUDY	New managing partner – 90 lawyers in firm
How have you found your first few months as managing partner?	An interesting challenge.
Which aspects have been difficult?	Although I had a pretty in-depth knowledge of the workings of the firm and had been supportive of the strategy (which obviously helped), we had only completed the appointment of our new professional management team very shortly prior to my own appointment. One key challenge has been to encourage them to develop their own ideas and practices to the advantage of the firm, whilst, at the same time, trying to convince the partners of the value our non-lawyer managers are adding.
	We do have an ambitious agenda and the most difficult aspect has been to try not to lose sight of the firm's overall strategy in the face of the time-consuming issues that need to be resolved on a day-to-day basis!

| How are you balancing fee earning with management? | Prior to my appointment we did have a period of about three months of handover (which I would recommend as a minimum). This did allow me to get up to speed on current issues affecting the firm generally and deal with the transfer of the bulk of my fee earning work in a reasonably orderly fashion. |

The size of the firm allows me to manage, for the majority of my time, although I think it important to be seen to be making a contribution at a fee earning level, not least to demonstrate to my partners that I still understand what it's like at the 'coal face'. Most fee-paying clients reasonably expect that their matters should take priority and this can sometimes be difficult to achieve. Where I continue to work on client matters, those clients have been made aware of my new position and, without exception, they have been very understanding.

| What percentage of your time is spent on management? | It varies from day to day but 90% on average. |

CASE STUDY   **New managing partner – 94 lawyers in firm**

| How have you found your first few months as managing partner? | I have found that the hardest aspect of becoming managing partner has been managing change. |

| Which aspects have been difficult? | Managers and fellow partners have found it relatively easy to accept me as the new managing partner. As far as staff are concerned I appear to have been well received. However, as the new managing partner my methods, emphasis, direction, priorities and decisions |

are different. Some of my partners have found this difficult to accept and, on occasion, I have found that old decision-making processes have been maintained despite my new role. Managing my partners through the change has required much tact, trust and diplomacy.

Actually, I love it all!!

| How are you balancing fee earning with management? | I am now fee earning at a level of 20% of my time (and reducing). |

The subsequent years – fulfilling the role successfully

In most firms, but especially those that are larger, communication is at the heart of successfully performing the role of managing partner.

A very good starting point is to be visible, and get out and see your staff on a daily basis. One managing partner commented:

> Each day I will speak to perhaps 90 of our staff – I visit each department, and admittedly I am becoming the king of the one-liner, but at least they see me. I feel in touch.

Communications can be face to face, in meetings and by e-mail:

> Communications. Use e-mail a lot, but have to avoid debate by e-mail. Have rule of no more than three e-mails, then talk. E-mail can be effective in getting message over to a large number of people. Need to exercise judgement in what is communicated, when and to whom. Default is to communicate everything about the business. Last year we had a series of eight staff meetings, this year gave each member of staff a DVD.

> Make all your communications relevant. Keep referring back to the business plan. Drip-feed the plan the whole time.

What topics should be communicated?
- Financial – hitting targets
- Good news – can sometimes hide bad news amongst the good news
- Marketing – we send a 'Marketing Week' round the whole firm.

> I maintain a list of all my partners and when I speak to each of them. I make sure I see all individually at least once a month. Very valuable to have coffee with someone.

Some firms are willing to embrace innovative ideas to support their partners and staff:

> Can be heavy direct and indirect costs associated with mental health and stress. When a legal executive became ill it made us realise the even higher cost of an equity partner becoming ill. We provide a lot of training in people management skills – even at low levels – so people can be aware of signs of stress. We have a Well Person check-up every 18 months for partners. All partners have a session with a psychologist and all staff have free access on an anonymous basis. Better to involve psychologist early on. Resource has made huge difference.

The managing partner's real strength generally lies in their ability to create a good tier of management at team or departmental manager level – as discussed in the next chapter.

Passing on the baton – life after being managing partner

The issue of succession is sometimes difficult as a managing partner reaches the end of their second, or perhaps third, term. Traditionally, the plan has often been to do the job for six or nine years and then return full-time to fee earning, perhaps at the same time taking on the role of senior partner. Unfortunately it is not always that easy. Two main problems can arise.

The first flows from the greater need, especially in larger firms, for the job to be full-time, and that has resulted in many managing partners losing their previously close relationships with their clients and becoming out of touch with the law. It can, in those circumstances, be difficult to re-build a client base, in particular when you may previously have been one of your firm's highest fee earners. It is especially difficult in firms that focus too much on personal fee levels. It is easy to lose confidence.

The second problem arises from the fact that some managing partners find they like management more than fee earning, and are probably better at it.

It is fairly important, then, for managing partners to review at intervals during their term of office their longer-term career plans and to ensure they are able to return to fee earning if they wish. Although a managing partner may be full-time, in practice it is always better still to be carrying a small workload – perhaps 20% – and retaining a small number of clients. Perhaps the most useful person a managing partner can have (in addition to an excellent PA or secretary) is a good assistant, a reliable solicitor who works with them dealing with the detail of their client work whilst they manage the firm.

The relationship with the clients will change and will be less 'hands on', but there may be one or two where you are still involved in the detail so as to keep up to date with the law.

It is especially useful to acquire the occasional new client because one of the problem areas can be a lack of confidence in winning new clients on returning to fee earning. In reality, if you have been able to use your time as managing partner effectively, you will have become a far better marketer and will have been moving in a much higher circle of contacts than previously, and should be able to use this to your advantage.

With careful planning, therefore, it should be possible to return to fee earning, albeit in a different role and different level. The increased work-getting potential of an ex managing partner should in particular not be understated – you will have made contacts that are invaluable to you and to the firm as a whole, and will now have time to exploit them.

SUMMARY

- The managing partner is a key ingredient to the success of most successful firms.
- Ensure the role is clear.
- Make sure you have sufficient time to perform the role.
- Deal with difficult or under-performing partners – don't duck the issue.
- Start developing your successor at an early stage.
- Always have in mind your exit route – what you will do after being managing partner.

Notes

1   Autumn Forum – Calcot Manor, Gloucestershire – Otterburn Legal Consulting.

2   If you are concerned that one of your partners (or indeed any of your solicitors) is suffering from stress or depression, alcohol or drug abuse, has an eating disorder or any other health problem, you can contact LawCare for confidential advice on 0800 279 6888 or email them at **admin@lawcare. org.uk**. Their website is **www.lawcare.org.uk**. The Solicitors Assistance Scheme (SAS) may also be able to help – their number is 020 7320 5795 and their website is **www.solicitorsassistancescheme.org.uk**.

Michael Shaw, managing partner – Cobbetts LLP, Manchester, Leeds and Birmingham

How long have you been managing partner for?	11 years.
How many partners and lawyers does your firm have?	Partners: 107; other fee earners: 300.
How would you describe your firm (top 100, high street, publicly funded etc. . .)?	Regional.
What percentage of your time is spent on management?	100%
How did you find your first few months as managing partner?	Relatively straightforward – it has become more complicated as we have grown (both organically and by acquisition).
What are the best parts of the job?	The people and having the ability to try to create something for the future.
What are the hardest parts of the job?	Ensuring that we don't throw the baby out with the bathwater as we realise our ambitions.
How do you balance fee earning with management?	N/a
Any tips on motivating fellow partners and providing leadership?	Trying to be aware of communication failure, remembering that it is a two-way process.
How do you see the role of departmental/team leaders?	Settling a collective ambition for their departments within the context of our firm-wide objectives.
What qualities would you look for in your successor?	Emotional intelligence first and foremost.
What advice would you give your successor?	Having listened to those around you, trust your instincts.
Would you consider a non-lawyer chief executive as your successor?	Yes. An insider (who is not a lawyer) who is of the right calibre may well have the advantage because of the knowledge they will have

accumulated and the strength of relationships which they enjoy.

Any other thoughts?

I know one or two non-lawyer chief executives; their success in the role is down to very great ability. It's hard enough as a lawyer to persuade other lawyers that you understand their problems so I really admire them.

7

Of equal importance – team and departmental management

The importance of line management

The managing partner provides overall leadership and direction, but it is down to the individual team and departmental managers to make it happen. Working with the managing partner, they are central to achieving change within a firm.

Team and departmental managers become ever more important as firms increase in size. Even in smaller firms the managing partner may not see all the fee earners of the firm on a regular basis:

> Our managing partner is a great guy – I don't see him that often – he is in the family department, I am in personal injury. They are actually in the next building, on the second floor – we are on the first floor of the annex – I don't see him that often, but when I do he is great, and asks how we are getting on.

The larger the firm, the less the managing partner will see individual lawyers and staff. Apart from the very exceptional managing partner, he or she may not even know their names. The people with the real influence, who can change behaviour, are the team or departmental leaders, who will speak to the members of their teams on a daily basis.

Poor managers

A poor manager can have a terrible impact on a team's performance and sense of team spirit:

> She showed clear favouritism and fought for salary increases for the fee earners she liked. She actually opposed increases for everyone else – it was really just spite, and a very petty attitude. Rather childlike in showing favouritism.

I asked a group of young solicitors attending training courses for junior partners / team leaders to describe their experience of poor managers:

Poor managers . . .

- Are often unmotivated themselves
- Can be inaccessible
- Give little praise
- Rarely lead by example
- Would criticise in public
- Did not deal with problems
- Could be defensive
- Were not team players
- Disorganised
- Had favourites

Good managers

The same people were asked to describe the characteristics of good managers that they had worked for. The answers were quite different:

Good managers . . .

- Listened
- Had humour
- Led by example
- Protected their team
- Celebrated success
- Were good communicators
- Were interested
- Well organised
- Good role model
- Inspired loyalty
- Fought your corner
- Gave praise
- Trust
- Decisive
- Genuine
- Thoughtful

The real shame was that some had never actually had a good manager – all they could do was describe the characteristics of what they thought a good manager should be like.

Residential conveyancing team leader – four lawyers plus nine support staff

How long have you been team leader for?	Six years.
What percentage of your time is spent on management as opposed to fee earning?	20%
Do you have personal fee targets? If so, is yours reduced to reflect your management role?	Yes, but no reduction is offered to me for being team leader.
How would you describe your role? What are the key aspects of your job?	My role is to run the team effectively and profitably, to look at the longer-term issues of team development and recruitment, to oversee marketing issues and to be a sounding board for team members for everything from business to personal issues.
Who do you report to? Do you have much contact with that person?	I report to the managing partner.
What makes a good team leader?	Patience.
Any tips for your successor?	Listen to everyone – they all have something to say. Do not try and reinvent the wheel overnight. Large groups of people take time to turn around.

Defining the role

As in the case of managing partner, the first stage of getting line management right in a firm is to define the role.

A team leader job description could be along the lines of:

1. Responsible for:

    (a) Day-to-day management of their department
    (b) Seeking to achieve the department's profit budget
    (c) The staff in their department
    (d) Leading the department's marketing
    (e) House-keeping in the department – in particular, file closing and clearing any balances
    (f) Minimising department work in progress (WIP), unpaid bills and unpaid disbursements
    (g) Standard of work in department (including speed of work being typed)
    (h) Lexcel, money laundering and other compliance within department

2. Accountable to managing partner
3. Team/department heads should meet briefly monthly (may need to be weekly, depending on situation) with each lawyer to confirm fee forecast for coming month and any problem matters
4. Team/department heads would chair monthly meetings of all lawyers in team. Support staff attend every other month

Having defined the role it is important to give the person time to carry it out. Assuming the person was already busy as a lawyer in the team, there is no point giving them the additional workload and responsibility of team leader without reducing their chargeable time or fee targets accordingly.

CASE STUDY   **Litigation team leader – 90 lawyers plus 30 support staff**

How long have you been team leader for?	Eight years as team leader; four years as practice area head.
What percentage of your time is spent on management as opposed to fee earning?	65%

Do you have personal fee targets?	Yes.
If so, is yours reduced to reflect your management role?	Yes, 50%.
How would you describe your role?	Manager of seven team leaders of litigation teams reporting to managing partner for litigation.
What are the key aspects of your job?	Financial control, practice development, HR.
Who do you report to?	Managing partner.
Do you have much contact with that person?	Monthly one-to-one meetings. Bi-monthly practice area head meetings.
What makes a good team leader?	Listener, analyst, motivator.
Any tips for your successor?	Do it in your own style.

Managers also need to be very conscious that lawyers will focus on whatever is measured and reported on. If a firm has a focus on fees, in particular individual fees, it would only be human nature to ensure your own fees are respectable. In these firms the team leader may be protective of his or her own fees, as will other members of the team. The team members may work alongside each other, they may share the same secretaries, but they will not work together as a team. If by contrast, greater emphasis is placed on team fee targets, completely different behaviour can result. The team leader may be much more willing to distribute work so that it is actually done by the correct person, and people may more easily work together on matters. The team leader will not feel the same need to justify his or her existence by the fees he or she bills personally.

The qualities of a good team leader are very similar to those of a good managing partner:

- a listener;
- good people skills;

- energy;
- someone who can instil trust and respect;
- someone who will take decisions;
- a business builder.

The role is very akin to being managing partner of that part of the firm.

CASE STUDY	**Commercial and corporate finance team leader – eight lawyers and four support staff**
What percentage of your time is spent on management as opposed to fee earning?	Varies, but on average I would say about 15–20% on management (including marketing the team).
Do you have personal fee targets? If so, is yours reduced to reflect your management role?	Yes. Yes, by approximately 25%.
How would you describe your role? What are the key aspects of your job?	Chairman of team meetings, with responsibility for running the agenda and most of the content; keeping an eye on financial performance of the team and individuals within it, including reviewing individual fee, WIP and debtor figures; leading marketing initiatives for the team; liaison with director of personnel regarding recruitment and personnel issues within the team. Fee earning.
Who do you report to? Do you have much contact with that person?	Head of department. Monthly face-to-face meetings. Also a written report is provided to the board on a monthly basis.

| What makes a good team leader? | Good financial discipline in order to set an example; positive attitude to the team and its efforts, encouraging rather than criticising; open mind about new initiatives and methods of working; strength to address poor performance in a constructive manner where required, rather than ignoring it or brushing it under the table. |
| Any tips for your successor? | Don't neglect management issues in favour of fee earning – ensure time is set aside to prepare for team meetings and ensure action points are followed up. |

SUMMARY

- In most firms, team or departmental leaders have greater contact with lawyers and support staff than the managing partner does, and are therefore key to achieving change.
- The managing partner provides the overall direction, but effective line management is needed to make it happen.
- The qualities needed of team leaders are very similar to those of a managing partner – they are the managing partner of their part of the business.
- Team leaders must be given time to undertake their role.

Helen Johnson, managing partner – Emery Johnson, Leicester

How long have you been managing partner for?	Approximately two years.
How many partners and lawyers does your firm have?	Three equity partners, two associates, six solicitors, five paralegals/trainees.
How would you describe your firm (top 100, high street, publicly funded etc. . .)?	Niche practice covering all family and criminal law. Largely legal aid.
What percentage of your time is spent on management?	Approximately 30%.
How did you find your first few months as managing partner?	Prior to becoming managing partner I had been in effect doing the job, so it was good to have it acknowledged. I felt more able to make decisions without constantly getting everyone's views first.
What are the best parts of the job?	The satisfaction of having a well-managed practice and happy staff. Feeling that I have the information I need to move things forward.
What are the hardest parts of the job?	On occasions it can be isolating and overwhelming if you are dealing with a difficult situation. Putting plans in place for future development when the future for legal aid is so uncertain.
How do you balance fee earning with management?	This is a constant issue. Due to the fact that I deal with criminal law the court commitments have to take precedence but when I am in the office I often feel I don't get any fee earning done and a lot of it gets done at night at home.
	I did start off with a set day a week for management but now I just fit it all in as and when I can.
Any tips on motivating fellow partners and providing leadership?	You need always to be aware that how you behave affects the firm. You cannot afford to have a bad day. You

always need to remain professional. It is important to be open to ideas and ultimately partners need to be loyal to each other and respect each other's strengths.

How do you see the role of departmental/team leaders?

Ideally the team leaders should deal with day-to-day management of the department, i.e. allocation of work, monitoring of performance and dealing with minor issues within the department. They also need to be an ambassador for the department and set an example to their department in terms of providing a high quality, professional service to clients.

What qualities would you look for in your successor?

Someone with a vision for the future who is able to deal with change and conflict in a controlled manner. Someone who the staff respect and look to for leadership. Someone dynamic but diplomatic.

What advice would you give your successor?

Never be afraid to ask for help from fellow partners or outside professionals. When implementing new changes accept that this will lead to disquiet and work hard to reassure staff. Remember that the little gestures are worth a lot and that good staff are you most valuable asset.

Would you consider a non-lawyer chief executive as your successor?

There is no reason why a managing partner has to be a lawyer but he or she needs to understand the pressure of fee earning and managing which others in the firm will have to balance.

Any other thoughts?

Being a managing partner is a challenge but it is also very rewarding, particularly when you get positive feedback and things are going well. When things are going less well you feel the pressure. As a lawyer without management training it has been a huge learning curve setting up a business and managing it but I am proud of what I have achieved and I believe that, provided you are open to ideas, prepared to read relevant books, publications and attend management seminars, you can do a good job. Traditionally lawyers have been bad at recognising the value of good management but that is changing and the firms that survive the challenges ahead will do so because of good management and not just because they are good lawyers.

8

Professional managers

Increasingly the most successful firms are in part successful due to their ability to attract and retain professional managers – people who are not lawyers by training, who have often experienced a very different business life elsewhere. This trend is likely to accelerate over the coming years.

Many managing partners will see these professional managers as absolutely key to the ability of their firms to succeed. They can be as important as many of the partners – more important in many instances. Their contribution has been key to the success of some firms.

The benefits of non-lawyer managers

As firms evolve and grow in size, partners invariably spend an ever-greater proportion of their time on management, some completely giving up the law. As they develop they normally move from employing a cashier, to recruiting a practice manager, and then on to employing professional managers – initially often in finance, followed by personnel, marketing and IT. Invariably a point is reached where it is suggested the firm should appoint a chief executive.

High quality professional managers are central to the release of partner time from day-to-day management, and also to improving the quality of that management.

The appointment of a professional manager should be undertaken in the light of an overall review of the firm's management structure and should aim to:

- improve the quality of the firm's management and administration;
- free partner time from unnecessary involvement in administration.

When considering such an appointment, do not underestimate the potential benefits a good person can deliver, and do not try to economise on the salary package offered. There are relatively few good people around, so don't risk losing a good person by paying too little.

Good people are always at a premium and as a practice you have to make a very important decision. If you simply require an administrator then go and get one. If, like many smaller firms, you actually want someone who can do the administration, but will also bring other significant skills to the party you must consider paying the price it takes to get the right person. As when recruiting lawyers, if you pay average money, you get an average person. There are wider economic implications linked to full employment. With professional staff in whatever sector in short supply, rightly or wrongly, if you don't pay the right money you are unlikely to get the right person.[1]

Professional managers can be grouped under four broad headings:

- cashiers;
- practice managers;
- support directors: directors of HR, finance, IT and marketing;
- chief executives.

Cashiers

Most smaller firms will employ a cashier, however their role is normally simply to maintain the books, post transactions, prepare the salaries, etc.

A good cashier who understands the accounts rules requirements is an essential requirement for any firm. You need to have confidence that this is under control. It is important that your cashier is qualified and receives good technical support, and your cashier should be encouraged to join a professional body such as the Institute of Legal Cashiers and Administrators.[2]

CASE STUDY   **Senior legal cashier – manages two members of staff**

Who do you report to?   Senior partner.

How would you describe your role? What are the key aspects of your job?   Financial control. Bank reconciliations, production of monthly management accounts. Liaise with partners re financial position. Legal aid reconciliations. Etc., etc.

What qualities do you look for in a managing partner?	Financial awareness, people management skills, control and organisational skills. Fair and consistent judgement.
How do you find dealing with lawyers?	Often like banging head against a brick wall. Lack of interest in financial matters. They give the impression of superiority and that the cashiers' problems are not theirs.
Any tips for managing them successfully?	Initially the management must come from the partners, who should be seen to be complying with certain standards and procedures. They should be instructed to cooperate with cashiers.
What makes a good support director / manager?	Again – good people management skills and organisational skills. Being able to communicate the importance of tasks.
Any tips for your successor?	When setting up new procedures ensure that all fee earners are aware of the importance of cooperation. Use the senior partners to help establish your role within the firm.

In small firms the cashier will spend much of their time posting transactions during the month, running the payroll, dealing with suppliers, producing month-end print-outs, chasing overdue debtors, dealing with computer problems, VAT, PAYE, etc., etc. It is a time-consuming and often frustrating job. A cashier rarely gets involved in the wider management of the firm – mainly due to a lack of time. The first step for many smaller firms to improve their management, therefore, is to recruit a practice manager.

Practice manager

Many firms appoint a practice manager, often in addition to the cashier, to undertake a much wider management role, often including staff issues, IT and virtually anything else the partners ask them to get involved in.

Practice manager – 10 members of staff

Who do you report to?	Principal.
How would you describe your role? What are the key aspects of your job?	Day-to-day running of the administration of the office, accounts department (including the sourcing and purchasing for the business), preparation of financial statements and quarterly management accounts, reconciling the bank accounts, client and office, on a monthly basis. Staff welfare (HR), IT, new employee induction etc., organising courses for principal and fee earners ensuring that they are up to date with their CPD. The running of the property. PA to principal.
What qualities do you look for in a managing partner?	Firm but fair with a good sense of humour!
How do you find dealing with lawyers?	As I am an accountant by profession and tend to deal in a logical fashion it can be frustrating at times, but on the whole enjoyable.
Any tips for managing them successfully?	Be firm when you need something done (and sometimes let them think the idea came from them).
What makes a good support director / manager?	Patience, being cool-headed when a problem arises and know your job and never be afraid to ask for help. We are continually learning. Have an open-door policy.
Any tips for your successor?	Be a good listener, realise that the universe does not revolve around your department and follow the above.

Sometimes the cashier develops into the role of practice manager; in other instances it is someone without any accountancy training. Once again the problem can be that everything is 'dumped' on this person and they soon sink under an impossible range of duties.

CASE STUDY	Practice manager – 40 members of staff
Who do you report to?	Managing partner.
How would you describe your role? What are the key aspects of your job?	My role contains all jobs that are non-legal within the practice. Key aspects include all HR (contracts, recruitment and selection, discipline, counselling), marketing, management accounts, IT and business development.
What skills do you look for in a managing partner?	Management skills! An ability to delegate and get the most out of people.
How do you find dealing with lawyers?	Difficult! They are highly opinionated and find it difficult to accept advice and criticism.
Any tips for managing them successfully?	Find a good managing partner and let him or her take the credit for any management that occurs; they seem to take advice better from another lawyer.
What makes a good support director / manager?	Memory. Ability to be pulled from one job to another to another and have recollection of a job half-finished from the month before. Being able to influence lawyers, usually by letting them think that they have made all the decisions!
Any tips for your successor?	Negotiate your job function and salary before you start! Do not take on all jobs that the partners suggest!

The starting point for appointing a practice manager, and for getting it right from the outset, is to be clear about the role and to prepare a realistic job description.

As firms become larger the job reaches a point where the role of practice manager must be split. In a single-office firm with, say, 10 partners and a total of 60 or 70 people, the administration of the firm may come under two people: the accountant and the practice manager. Both would report to the managing partner.

The staff in cashiers would report to the accountant, who would be responsible for:

- monthly and quarterly accounts;
- VAT, PAYE, etc.;
- dealing with suppliers;
- posting accounting transactions;
- petty cash;
- salaries;
- IT back-up;
- closing old files, and the billing of certain areas of work.

The receptionists, office juniors and cleaners would report to the practice manager. Secretaries would report to their head of department, but the practice manager would deal with all staff problems relating to secretarial and support staff. He or she would be responsible for:

- staff records and personnel;
- temporary staff;
- holidays;
- stationery;
- recruitment of secretaries and support staff;
- authorisation of any overtime by support staff;
- IT maintenance and technical problems;
- marketing support.

In this type of arrangement both the accountant and practice manager would meet with the managing partner at least weekly and would often form part of the management team running the firm on a day-to-day basis.

Practice manager – 13 members of staff

Who do you report to?	Four partners.
How would you describe your role? What are the key aspects of your job?	Financial management. Insurance. IT. Overseeing all aspects of the firm from staff contracts to negotiating overheads.
What skills do you look for in a managing partner?	Organised and helpful. Willing to be involved in the running of the firm. Decisive.
How do you find dealing with lawyers?	At times frustrating but if you work hard and successfully manage the firm well, then no problem at all.
Any tips for managing them successfully?	Be patient and firm with them but not too firm so they think you are telling them what to do. Explain the essential facts and don't over-complicate matters.
What makes a good support director / manager?	Confident and good communicator. Able to assess a situation and use initiative quickly to solve problems.
Any tips for your successor?	Don't do a better job than me!

In order to get maximum benefit from the appointment of a practice manager, bear the following points in mind:

- **Spend quite a bit of time getting the job description right.** Don't give the person an absolutely impossible set of tasks to do because they will fail.

- **Be clear what the actual scope of the job is.** Are you looking for a kind of 'super cashier' who will actually spend most of their time on day-to-day cashiering, or do you want someone who will perform more of a management role?
- **Be clear who the person is going to report to.** It is not possible to report to all 10 partners, even though you may run your firm as an equal partnership. Specify the person the practice manager is going to report to and agree their authority limits.

Support directors

As firms get larger they invariably move beyond the stage where one person can fulfil the practice manager role, and professionals in each of the main areas are appointed.

Typically the first appointment is an accountant, partnership secretary or director of finance, followed often by personnel, marketing and IT professionals.

At this size of firm, fewer mistakes tend to be made concerning the job specification, however issues can arise around reporting structures, and whether there is still a need to have a staff or marketing partner. This type of appointment normally works well. There are issues, but the basic concept of the job has been thought through and they have a clear brief.

CASE STUDY	**Director of HR – 25 in team, 160 people in firm**
Who do you report to?	Managing partner.
How would you describe your role? What are the key aspects of your job?	1. Director of personnel looking after the needs of the firm, strategic planning, selection and recruitment, induction, training needs and ensuring employment law legislation is complied with, including implementing, monitoring and evaluating procedures and policies. 2. Head of the admin team – leading all support staff, coordinating and ensuring complete office support on both of our sites.

What qualities do you look for in a managing partner?	Someone who leads by example, who is well organised, firm but fair – someone prepared to listen and evaluate but at the same time is prepared to take difficult decisions and stand by them; someone who can gain the confidence and respect of others.
How do you find dealing with lawyers?	A breed of their own! The important thing is to get to know them and win their confidence – once they know they can trust you, that you will do what you say and that you are fair and objective, they will be happy to delegate and seek your guidance.
Any tips for managing them successfully?	Respect them and accept that they are all individuals who need handling in a slightly different way. Offer support and advice but let them think it is their idea!
What makes a good support director / manager?	Good communication – someone who is respected, leads by example, is approachable and who understands the business needs.
Any tips for your successor?	Get a thorough understanding of the business and what is expected of staff: care for them – empathise, listen, support and counsel when required. Be proactive and well organised.

Chief executives

The next stage of development beyond appointing professionals in charge of functional areas such as finance and marketing is to appoint a 'chief executive' to run the firm.

A growing number of firms have considered this option as a solution to the partners' own lack of management training, however it has been successful so far in relatively few instances. It very much depends on finding the right person – and in particular being willing to pay an appropriate salary to get the right person – and the partners being ready to relinquish control.

An added difficulty, especially in smaller firms, is that partners often need a chief executive who is entrepreneurial in outlook – he or she needs to be a risk taker. At present many of the people who might apply for these positions are not risk takers – they are administrators. The result can easily be disappointment and frustration on the part of both the partners and the chief executive. A good test is to ask whether, subsequent to the Legal Services Bill, he or she will be willing to invest his or her own money in the firm – if there is hesitation in their answer they may well not be the right person.

A further problem is that the partners of many firms are simply not ready for this type of appointment. The former managing partner of one firm who had appointed a chief executive about a year previously, made the point very clearly that his partners had only reached the point in the previous couple of years where they were ready to accept someone from outside. Over the previous four years the partners had been involved progressively less in management decisions, as more and more responsibility had been taken on by the managing partner and his team. They had therefore adjusted to not being actively involved. He felt that if that had not happened the attempt to introduce a chief executive would have been a disaster.

If you get these various factors right then a chief executive can work well – just make sure you are ready, that you are clear about the role, and are willing to release control.

SUMMARY

- **Professional managers are playing a growing role in the management of many firms.**
- **Beware of creating an impossible job description for a practice manager.**
- **If you pay an average salary you will get an average person – pay what it takes to get someone who will add value to the firm.**
- **Support directors can make a real contribution to the management of a firm.**
- **The appointment of a chief executive actually to run the firm has to be approached with care. The partners need to be ready and you must be willing to pay what may seem a very high salary to get the right person.**

Notes

1   Chris Denington – Zinc Legal 0207 419 6411.
2   The ILCA can be contacted at 0208 302 2867. Their website is **www.ilca. org.uk.**

Andy Duxbury, chief executive – Aaron & Partners LLP, Chester and Manchester

How long have you been chief executive for?	Since August 2006.
How many partners and lawyers does your firm have?	As at end April 2007, 18 partners and 32 other fee earners.
How would you describe your firm (top 100, high street, publicly funded etc. . .)?	Commercial firm – striving to build a regional presence in the North West and North Wales.
What is your background? Are you a lawyer?	Background entirely in marketing and business development – 20 years in industry (e.g. Boots, car rental sector and RAC Motoring Services amongst others); three-and-a-half years as marketing director for a leading South West firm; three-and-a-half years as business development director at a leading Manchester firm.
How did you find your first few months as chief executive?	Exciting and liberating. Suddenly I was involved with everything and was given great freedom to operate. (The previous managing partner was only too glad to move things off his desk!) I was particularly tasked with updating/developing a new business plan for the firm and the partners encouraged me to start with a blank piece of paper.
	At the same time, I clearly embarked on a steep learning curve in relation to some of the areas I was now responsible for. It's one thing to sit in a management meeting at a large firm discussing the issues – it's a whole new ball game when it's you who has to make the decision, get on with implementing it and deal with the problems that might arise.
What are the best parts of the job?	In relation to Aaron & Partners' current situation, it has to be driving forward the strategy – leading from

	the front, making it happen. Taking the lead in conducting merger discussions with potential partners, as we looked to move into Manchester, has been a new and hugely exciting experience. The first of these meetings was when it really hit home that I was truly in a position of responsibility.
What are the hardest parts of the job?	Nothing new here, I suspect. It has to be partner compliance – converting the acceptance/agreement of what needs to be done into action.
How do you find dealing with lawyers?	Mentally, it's tough. I find you always need to be on the top of your game in dealing with the questioning and challenging. I'm fortunate at Aaron & Partners that no one is 'subversive' (I've seen it elsewhere!) but it can be hard work to keep things moving forward. In my experience of law firms, a small but significant minority always attempt to re-visit decisions already made and re-write history!
	It's also frustrating that many lawyers are incapable of dealing with the minor issues – usually HR-related. Bizarrely, many of them shy away from confrontation.
Any tips for managing them successfully?	Anything substantive that needs doing has to be explained and justified up front. You can't 'tell' lawyers what to do, you always have to prepare the 'how's' and 'why's' in advance.
	However, once you've got your arguments prepared, then you need to be decisive and take the lead in making things happen. Once lawyers have 'bought in', they want to be led (in my view).
Any tips on motivating the partners and providing leadership?	It may be peculiar to Aaron & Partners, but I've found the key thing is to be very visible and involved. It's important to be open, to engage in what each partner/team is up to, to 'walk the floors' constantly.

I also feel – and it's something we focused on in the new business plan – that you need to set clear goals and have real clarity about what is expected of each person.

How do you see the role of departmental/team leaders?

I see them having responsibility for four things:

(a) managing the performance of the people in their team – utilisation, billing, lock-up, etc.;

(b) ensuring quality and client service standards are followed;

(c) providing a channel or conduit for communication and engagement with the team;

(d) directing and leading business development activity (with assistance and support from marketing).

What qualities would you look for in your successor?

A clear business thinker, particularly relating to strategy; energetic and hands-on – a real 'do-er'; excellent and open communicator; resilient and persistent.

What advice would you give your successor?

Spend time getting to know everyone – walk the floors; create forums for two-way communication; strive for 'engagement'.

Don't try to operate in a vacuum – discuss and debate the issues with the equity partners and/or team leaders, but be decisive in taking action.

Particularly important for Aaron & Partners, at its present stage of development, is for the CEO to have a significant external role – so a commercial awareness is key. I'm a great believer in the maxim that you have to truly know about business and the business.

Any other thoughts?

It's vitally important to have clear parameters for the role. You cannot afford to be constrained and only 'following orders'.

9

The senior partner and other partners' roles in management

As indicated in the previous three chapters, the managing partner, team or departmental leaders and support directors are increasingly likely to be the main driving forces in the management of most law firms.

The other partners, in particular in smaller firms, can still, however, have a huge part to play. The key is to make the most of everyone's strengths. What are people good at?

Finance, marketing, HR and IT partners

A number of areas need to be managed in order for a firm to function on a day-to-day basis, and these are normally grouped under a number of headings:

- finance;
- marketing;
- HR;
- IT.

There can be other headings (such as library, premises and insurance etc.) but the four listed above are the principal areas for most firms.

As firms grow, professionals may be appointed to lead and manage each of these areas, but initially, especially in smaller firms, these are likely to be dealt with by a partner. In very small firms the managing or senior partner may deal with all of these areas personally, perhaps assisted by various members of staff. Between these extremes individual partners normally head up each area reporting back to the partners' meeting or to a small executive.

As in the case of the managing partner, it is important to spell out the responsibilities of each role and to agree their authority.

Normally, at the start of each year, a budget should be agreed for each area, and responsibility for spending that budget would be vested in the appropriate partner. In practice he or she would normally consult and discuss ideas with others, but essentially that person should be in charge of the budget, and would only need to come back to the partners if it needed to be increased – or perhaps to explain major under-spends.

The senior partner

The role of senior partner is an important, sometimes neglected position in many firms of solicitors. Nowadays they are also not always that 'senior' – they are getting younger, and the concept of the job is changing.

Historically, most firms did not have a managing partner, and were instead managed and run, often very successfully, by their senior partner who took on a much more 'hands-on' and executive role than is generally seen today.

The management problems of a number of firms today have their roots in the retirement of these all-powerful figures who were sometimes very autocratic and often poor at developing and training their successors. In some instances the most likely successors had left over the years because very autocratic senior partners were often difficult to work with. In some instances they clashed with strong personalities below them and in others they simply stifled the development of the immediate level of partners below them. In some firms there is an age gap in the partnership: the natural successors to the senior partner are missing – and are instead running other firms nearby!

The result was, in many cases, partners who were happy to leave everything to the senior partner – sometimes to the detriment of his (or occasionally her) health, and who failed to learn and pick up the management skills and acumen they now need. Along the way they picked up an impression that management was more complicated than it actually is, and this sometimes fuels a feeling of inadequacy today.

These days many senior partners still play an important part in the development of their firms, however much of the day-to-day management has been passed to the managing partner, and also much of the strategic management also. The first task, therefore, is to define the role.

At one extreme, the job of senior partner, or chairman as it is often known, comprises simply:

- dealing with complaints;
- external projection of the firm – 'awarding the firm's prize at speech days of the local school';
- chairing partner meetings.

Others use the role in a more proactive way to complement and support the managing partner:

- someone whose job it is to think about the longer-term development of the firm – a 'brief to look at the longer term and chair our strategy committee';
- partner relations, or 'partners' partner';
- a sounding board.

Obviously the needs of firms will vary, however often this latter type of role is a very effective way of strengthening a firm's overall management and is a way of utilising the experience of more senior partners.

Traditionally the 'senior partner' was the first name on the letterhead, but this is changing. In a number of firms today the senior partner is an elected position – for a term of perhaps five years – and the people who fill the position are frequently retired managing partners. It is a tremendous way of capitalising on the skills and experience they learned whilst being managing partner. The average age is also coming down, from over 60 to mid 50s or 40s, or younger.

The senior partner and managing partner relationship

The relationship between senior and managing partner can sometimes be difficult to manage, but if it is a good relationship it can significantly boost the effectiveness of the managing partner. It can also make the job of managing partner much easier if he or she has a supportive senior partner.

The job of managing partner can sometimes be very lonely and the senior partner can be an invaluable sounding board, especially with regard to problems with fellow partners. The senior partner may well have been there before and will therefore have experience that can be drawn on.

The senior partner can also very usefully play the role of 'partners' partner' – someone the partners can turn to when they are not happy with how things are going. He or she can often diffuse a problem at an early stage and avoid a direct conflict with the managing partner.

Two quotes from the first edition of this book bear repetition:

CASE STUDY **Senior partner 1**

The senior partner has two key roles in our firm.

The first is the relationship within the management team where the senior partner must fulfil the role of a non-executive chairman and only get dragged into management issues when there is serious dissent or strong leadership is required to push through difficult decisions. The senior partner must not be regarded as the managing partner's echo and always there to support him against the world. The managing partner must earn the senior partner's support and accept that there are times when they will be at odds. Only in this way can the senior partner properly be seen as the 'partners' partner' throughout the firm.

Secondly, the external appearance of the relationship is important, both for the firm itself and for the outside world. The firm itself must understand that the managing partner is the CEO of the firm, whilst the senior partner is the father figure and ambassador who is wheeled out for all the usual state occasions and is the recognisable embodiment of the firm. So far as external relationships are concerned, the managing partner's role will be largely unseen as clients are not concerned about how the firm manages itself, as long as it does it properly. The senior partner will be more visible through his ambassadorial role.

CASE STUDY   **Senior partner 2**

I believe that the senior partner has an important role in a professional partnership not least because his position is quite different from that of the managing partner.

Whereas the managing partner must inevitably become immersed in the day-to-day affairs of the firm, the senior partner can (and should) detach himself and therefore has the ability to provide the overview. A good example of this is the role the senior partner can fulfil as chairman of partners' meetings and the management board. In these situations the managing partner will be seeking approval for a range of actions which relate to the driving forward and development of the business. Frequently he will be challenged and always he can be held to account. The senior partner (whilst clearly not working against the direction chosen by the managing partner) must allow issues to be properly debated and try to ensure a satisfactory outcome.

The senior partner should have the 'ear' of partners and staff. He should act as mentor and confidante and be regarded as the court of final appeal in relation to personnel issues. This contrasts with the position of the managing partner who will not be able to be at arm's length to such an extent.

The senior partner also has an important role to play both amongst the firm's clients and within the wider community. He has (or must create) the time to put himself about and to be seen as the face of the firm in public. The managing partner is likely to be too embroiled in the running of the firm to allow him to do this. More importantly, however, the senior partner, almost invariably, will have been around longer and will therefore be better suited to an ambassadorial role.

The second senior partner, who gave me this quote in 2002, is himself about to stand down and hand over to an elected chairman. I asked him to reflect on the last five years as senior partner:

I have very much enjoyed the role of senior partner which was something that I never expected to achieve. I think that each individual senior partner has their own style and mine inevitably has been different to that of my predecessor. I think it has been important to be in touch with all your colleagues across the patch and to be a good listener when needed which, in my case, has been quite often, particularly so with my partners. I see, not just in this firm but talking to colleagues from other firms, that the role is changing. I am to be replaced by one of my colleagues, as chairman, which is intended to reflect more the corporate structure of the firm in due course as an LLP.

However, his role will be limited to the extent that he will be chairing board and partners' meetings and, in addition, have a pastoral role. The role of complaints and MLRO (Money Laundering Reporting Officer) which I have also been responsible for will now become the responsibility of our managing partner. I imagine that my colleague may well carry out his role as chairman in a different manner to that which I am used to.

In some cases the relationship can be difficult, especially if the senior partner had previously been managing partner and had wanted to continue in that role. It is only human to feel annoyance and irritation when a successor comes in and changes things, but it is important, if the firm is to develop, not to frustrate things. It is especially important not to divide a partnership and work against a managing partner. The job often calls, therefore, for good interpersonal skills and a high degree of tact!

A senior partner or chairman is likely to chair some, but not necessarily all, partner meetings, but a working relationship has to be developed that does not sideline the managing partner at such meetings. A senior partner should ensure all partners have a chance to express their views and sometimes needs to elicit them. It is remarkable how many partners do not speak at partner meetings, yet these people will have views, and the silent partners who nod and agree at the meeting and then do nothing afterwards are a real problem in many firms. A good senior partner can help to bring these people out.

SUMMARY

- Make the most of the strengths of your partners – focus on what they are good at.
- Be very conscious that for all firms a point is reached where it becomes more effective for a professional manager to take over these roles from a partner.
- A senior partner or chairman within a firm can play an important role in supporting the managing partner and can result in an overall strengthening of the management of the firm.

Jay Bhayani,
senior partner –
Watson Esam, Sheffield

How long have you been senior partner for?	At Watson Esam we did not have designated titles of managing partner or senior partner but I feel that I have been in a leadership role for approximately seven years. We have recently formalised my role, and I am now senior partner.
How many partners and lawyers does your firm have?	Five partners, three non-partner solicitors and 10 other fee earners.
How would you describe your firm (top 100, high street, publicly funded etc. . .)?	General practice with niche areas of specialism.
What percentage of your time is spent on management?	Approximately 70%.
How did you find your first few months as senior partner?	The role evolved over time rather than commencing on a specific date. I joined the firm 15 years ago as a newly qualified solicitor, became a partner four years later and was involved in management of the firm from the outset, although this has become a much bigger part of my job over the last few years.
What are the best parts of the job?	Having more control over the direction the firm moves in and thinking strategically about the firm as a whole rather than just casework or my department.
What are the hardest parts of the job?	A feeling of loneliness sometimes, feeling a lack of enthusiasm or motivation from others whose main role is fee earning about initiatives which I feel benefit the firm.
How do you balance fee earning with management?	This was extremely difficult when the firm was smaller as I had to fit in the fee earning around the managing, usually in the evenings, as well as look after kids etc.! It is easier now as I have a team of fee earners who can deal with most of the fee earning work.

Any tips on motivating fellow partners and providing leadership?	Being enthusiastic and optimistic rubs off on others but also being quite frank about what is expected of other partners – impressing upon them the need to do more than just fee earn.
How do you see the role of departmental/team leaders?	Being less concentrated on fee earning themselves but ensuring those they manage and lead process work profitably – getting away from the idea of individual targets and thinking more like a department that has the same goal.
What qualities would you look for in your successor?	A high degree of confidence, the ability to inspire and motivate others, the ability to see and seize opportunities and think creatively, being personable, being resilient.
What advice would you give your successor?	To do things their own way, try new things, not feel they cannot deviate from my way as they may have a better or different approach.
Would you consider a non-lawyer chief executive as your successor?	Yes, if they have experience of a law firm.

Understanding the figures

10

The underlying factors that determine profitability

Profitability in England and Wales

As in previous years, there continues to be a wide variation in the profitability of firms of solicitors in England and Wales, as indicated in Figure 10.1. This figure illustrates the net profit per equity partner by size of firm in 2003, categorised according to the number of solicitors in the firm. This is the most recent Business Review published by the Law Society.

'Net profit' is defined as total income less total expenditure, and equates with the distributable profit as shown in a firm's accounts. 'Net profit per equity partner' is this total profit divided by the number of equity partners.

Each chart shows the median and also the upper and lower quartiles. The median is the middle value in the range and is not influenced by the

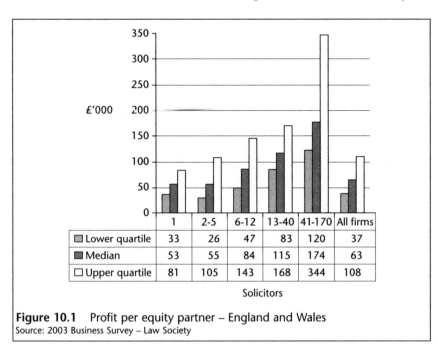

	1	2-5	6-12	13-40	41-170	All firms
☐ Lower quartile	33	26	47	83	120	37
■ Median	53	55	84	115	174	63
☐ Upper quartile	81	105	143	168	344	108

Solicitors

Figure 10.1 Profit per equity partner – England and Wales
Source: 2003 Business Survey – Law Society

extreme values (as the average is). The upper and lower quartiles indicate the range of values: 25% of firms are below the lower quartile and 25% of firms are above the upper quartile.

The figure indicates an overall median profit per equity partner in England and Wales in 2003 of £63,000, and that profitability increases with size of firm. As in previous years, within each size band there is also an enormous variation. In 25% of firms the equity partners earned under £37,000 each, compared to over £108,000 amongst the top 25%.

Figure 10.2 compares the median profits achieved by each size group in 2003 with those earned in 2001, and the chart indicates relatively strong profit growth over the two years.

Average profit per partner amongst the top 100 UK firms[1] was £408,000 in 2006, with average partner profit at Clifford Chance and Linklaters exceeding £1 million.

In 2003 the Department for Constitutional Affairs (DCA) commissioned research into the profitability of legal aid firms[2] as summarised in Figure 10.3. This indicates a median profit per equity partner of £63,000 – the same as the median for the profession as a whole at that time. Once again there was a wide spread of profits, with 25% of sole principals earning under £22,000 while other firms performed better, with 25% of firms achieving partner profits over £100,000.

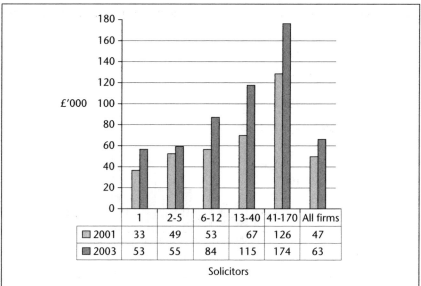

£'000	1	2-5	6-12	13-40	41-170	All firms
2001	33	49	53	67	126	47
2003	53	55	84	115	174	63

Solicitors

Figure 10.2 Median profit per equity partner – England and Wales – 2003 v 2001
Source: 2003 Business Survey – Law Society

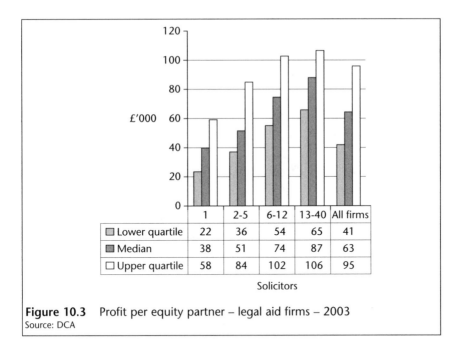

£'000	1	2-5	6-12	13-40	All firms
☐ Lower quartile	22	36	54	65	41
▨ Median	38	51	74	87	63
☐ Upper quartile	58	84	102	106	95

Solicitors

Figure 10.3   Profit per equity partner – legal aid firms – 2003
Source: DCA

Profitability in Scotland

Figure 10.4 summarises the profitability of firms in Scotland,[3] and a similar pattern is illustrated.

Two groups of firm are apparent – the large practices with more than 10 partners, and this will include some of the large commercial firms in both Edinburgh and Glasgow – and the rest of the profession, where profits are much lower.

Interestingly, in the firms with fewer than 10 equity partners, some of the most profitable firms are sole principals, especially in rural areas. A quarter of this latter group achieved profits over £125,000. They earn better profits because it is often difficult recruiting solicitors in rural areas – solicitors frequently prefer the cities – and the firms therefore have relatively low salaries bills. Some sole principals also work from home, and they often work very hard, sometimes to the detriment of their own health – but achieve good profits.

Figure 10.5 indicates the improvement that has taken place in profitability amongst Scottish firms in recent years. This is likely to reflect a buoyant economy in recent years, but may also be due to improved financial management on the part of the firms that take part in the survey, as many have participated for several years.

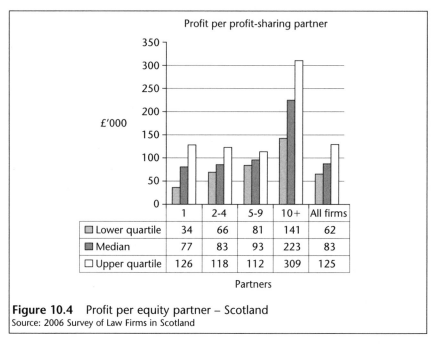

Profit per profit-sharing partner

£'000

	1	2-4	5-9	10+	All firms
▢ Lower quartile	34	66	81	141	62
▨ Median	77	83	93	223	83
▢ Upper quartile	126	118	112	309	125

Partners

Figure 10.4   Profit per equity partner – Scotland
Source: 2006 Survey of Law Firms in Scotland

The Business Review in England and Wales and the Law Society of
Scotland survey were both based on relatively large samples and are therefore statistically representative of their jurisdictions. The DCA survey was
also based on a reasonably large sample of around 270 firms, although
there was an overrepresentation of small crime firms.

The LMS Survey

Figure 10.6 illustrates the profit per partner achieved by the participants
in the Financial Benchmarking Survey 2005 published by the Law
Management Section (LMS).[4] This survey was based on completed questionnaires from 176 firms – approximately 10% of the LMS membership.
Although not representative of the profession as a whole, the firms in the
LMS Survey are more profitable than firms generally and are therefore a
good peer group to compare performance against. The Survey shows the
same increase in profitability with size and variation within each size
group.

Measuring profitability

Profit per equity partner is the most common way of measuring profitability amongst firms of solicitors. In many other sectors profit is

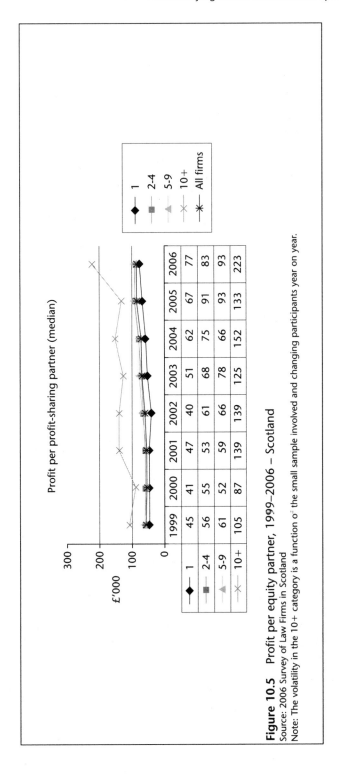

Profit per profit-sharing partner (median)

	1999	2000	2001	2002	2003	2004	2005	2006
1	45	41	47	40	51	62	67	77
2-4	56	55	53	61	68	75	91	83
5-9	61	52	59	66	78	66	93	93
10+	105	87	139	139	125	152	133	223

Figure 10.5   Profit per equity partner, 1999–2006 – Scotland
Source: 2006 Survey of Law Firms in Scotland
Note: The volatility in the 10+ category is a function of the small sample involved and changing participants year on year.

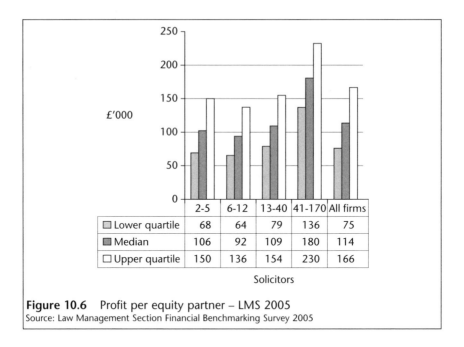

	2-5	6-12	13-40	41-170	All firms
☐ Lower quartile	68	64	79	136	75
▨ Median	106	92	109	180	114
☐ Upper quartile	150	136	154	230	166

Solicitors

Figure 10.6   Profit per equity partner – LMS 2005
Source: Law Management Section Financial Benchmarking Survey 2005

assessed in terms of a return on capital employed, however that has rarely been used in the legal sector as traditionally relatively little capital has been required – although this is something that may change in the future as a result of the Legal Services Bill.

The other measure that has frequently been used historically is net profit percentage – profit as a percentage of fees, and 30% has often been cited as a good figure to aim for. Figure 10.7 shows the average net profit percentage achieved by the most and least profitable firms in the LMS Survey – the firms achieving profits per partner above the upper quartile and below the lower quartile respectively and indicates that the most profitable firms still achieve a net profit percentage of around 25–30%.

The net profit percentage can, however, be a misleading measure, in particular amongst smaller firms, as it is possible to achieve a high net profit percentage but a low profit per equity partner – for example, in a firm that has too many equity partners.

As a management tool, the net profit percentage as calculated above is also of limited value as it excludes any cost for the equity partners – who, as partners, receive a share of the firm's profits, and are not therefore included in the firm's salaries as an employed solicitor would be. In particular, it is extremely difficult to compare departmental performance unless a notional salary is factored into the calculations for each equity partner.

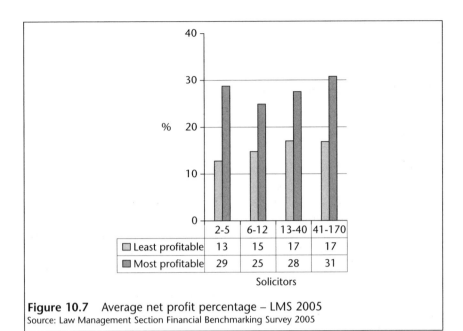

Figure 10.7   Average net profit percentage – LMS 2005
Source: Law Management Section Financial Benchmarking Survey 2005

Many firms therefore include a notional salary in their management accounts in respect of each equity partner – in their capacity as a lawyer or manager within their firm – as opposed to an owner or shareholder. In some cases a market rate will be determined for each partner, but more often a single figure is determined and applied to all the partners. This is often based on the salary of the highest-paid employed solicitor, perhaps a salaried partner, adding an amount, if appropriate, to reflect a partner's greater market value. This permits much better assessment of the performance of a team or department.

Increasingly, as new types of entity move into the legal sector and competition increases, firms will need to become even better at measuring profit and at assessing cost and will need to factor other 'hidden' costs into their calculations. These could include:

- a notional rent where the partners own the firm's offices and do not charge the practice a commercial rent;
- interest on partner capital account, in order to reflect a more accurate financing charge for the firm.

In order properly to assess performance these will need to be taken into account, and a net profit percentage calculated after these items is likely to be much more meaningful.

This issue, and the calculation, of the 'true' cost of services is discussed later in this part.

The key profitability drivers

The most obvious factors that could influence the profitability of firms of solicitors are:

- the quality of their client base, in particular its ability to generate a flow of repeat instructions;
- the complexity of the law being practised – clients will generally be willing to pay higher fees for real expertise;
- the size and value of the transaction, and the risk attached to it – once again clients have traditionally been willing to pay higher fees for significant transactions, and this is especially so in corporate finance and banking;
- the quality and technical ability of the lawyers undertaking the work – arguably clients will be willing to pay more for recognised experts in their fields;
- the work ethos of a firm – some people work harder and are more productive than others;
- size – the charts in this section all indicate larger firms are more profitable;
- an ability to control overheads and expenses.

These factors can be important and do impact upon profitability, however more significant profitability drivers are often:

- the firm's financial structure, in particular its level of gearing – the number of lawyers in addition to each equity partner;
- the number of equity partners amongst whom the firm's profits are shared;
- a small number of key performance indicators (KPIs) such as salaries and overheads relative to fees.

By developing the correct financial structure all the normal presumptions of profitability can be overturned. Firms undertaking low-margin work using lawyers of only standard ability can achieve high levels of profitability. These firms have developed a business model appropriate for the markets they operate in, and in particular have established a good financial structure. This is explored in more detail in the following chapters.

SUMMARY

- Profitability increases with size of firm.
- There is a wide variation in profitability within each size group.
- In order to assess performance it is necessary to factor in a cost for certain 'hidden' items. In particular, a notional salary for each equity partner, a notional rent on the firm's offices where these are owned by the partners, and a notional interest on partner capital.
- Whilst factors such as type of client base and the work undertaken do influence profitability, a firm's financial structure can be as important.

Notes

1   See www.thelawyer.com.
2   Otterburn, *Legal Consulting: Department for Constitutional Affairs – Review of Demand, Supply and Purchasing Arrangements – Survey of Legal Aid Firms* 2003.
3   Published by the Law Society of Scotland. The charts are analysed according to number of partners.
4   LMS Financial Benchmarking Survey 2005. In the original report, firms were analysed according to number of partners. In the charts used in this book the data has been re-analysed according to number of solicitors. Also, some corrections have been made to the original data, and some erroneous data excluded so the overall figures are slightly different to those previously published.

11

Gearing and revenue per partner

Gearing

Gearing is the number of other lawyers – solicitors, legal executives and paralegals – in addition to each equity partner. It is key to the profitability of most firms. The one exception is often niche specialist firms (in shipping, for example) where many of the lawyers could be partners; it is complex, high-value work that can be difficult to delegate. For most types of firm, however, it is generally difficult to achieve good profit levels if the equity partners are the main lawyers. In most cases profitability is better where there is good gearing, as illustrated by Figure 11.1, which analyses firms according to their profitability.

Figure 11.1 indicates that the most profitable firms tend to be ones where there are around six or seven lawyers in addition to each equity partner. If there are 10 equity partners there will therefore be a further 60 or 70 lawyers in the firm – solicitors, legal executives and paralegals.

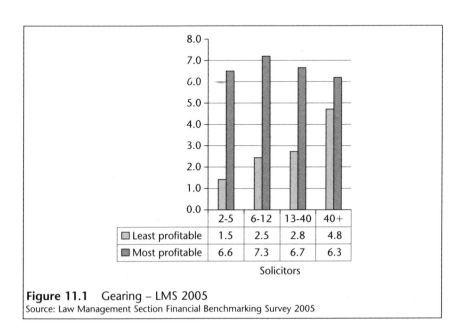

	2-5	6-12	13-40	40+
Least profitable	1.5	2.5	2.8	4.8
Most profitable	6.6	7.3	6.7	6.3

Solicitors

Figure 11.1   Gearing – LMS 2005
Source: Law Management Section Financial Benchmarking Survey 2005

As shown in Figure 11.2, a similar pattern was shown in the DCA survey in 2003 of legal aid firms: the firms achieving the highest profits had higher levels of gearing – except the sole practitioners that took part; in their case the most profitable curiously had lower levels of gearing. They would have earned most of the fees personally, and would have probably have had very low staff costs.

The position is similar in Scotland (see Figure 11.3) where, in 2006, the most profitable firms had approximately 2.5 other lawyers in addition to each equity partner.

The issue of gearing raises a wide range of questions concerning the type of work a firm does and who is actually going to do it. Good gearing is often much easier to achieve in some departments or areas of work than others. 'Volume' departments can achieve almost unlimited gearing, with one manager (not necessarily even a solicitor) running a department comprising a significant number of staff (often unqualified). This model is becoming more common.

An improvement in gearing is something that may take a number of years to achieve. It can be an elusive goal, and can be especially difficult for small firms where the partners are currently the main lawyers. In rural areas in particular it can be very difficult to recruit solicitors – many of the younger solicitors want to work in the commercial firms in the cities. If they do join a rural firm they want to be partners. This is as true in Scotland and Ireland as it is in England and Wales. They want to work in Edinburgh, in Glasgow, in Dublin; they want to work in London, in Cardiff, in Leeds, Manchester or Birmingham. The smaller the town a

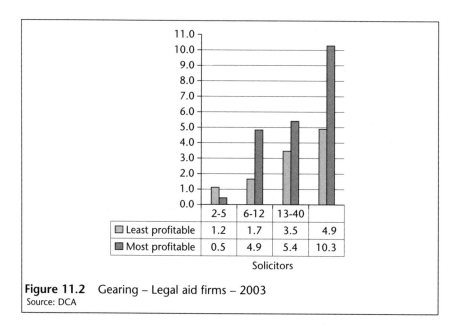

	2-5	6-12	13-40	
Least profitable	1.2	1.7	3.5	4.9
Most profitable	0.5	4.9	5.4	10.3

Solicitors

Figure 11.2   Gearing – Legal aid firms – 2003
Source: DCA

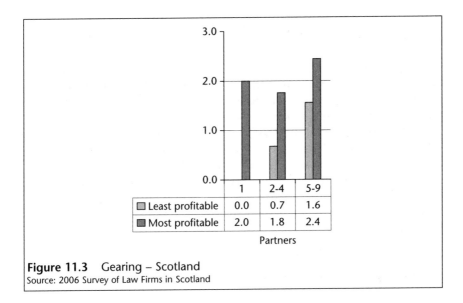

Figure 11.3 Gearing – Scotland
Source: 2006 Survey of Law Firms in Scotland

firm is based in, the more difficult it can be to recruit. Firms therefore have to be creative in their remuneration packages, and in the working environment and ethos that they offer. They also have to consider other levels of lawyer.

Future gearing should always be on the agenda when updating a firm's business plan. It needs to be considered at team or departmental level, and will be achieved by future partner retirements, combined with selective recruitment. Trainee solicitors can often be part of the solution, although there is always the danger that they will leave after qualification – once again, careful thought about the package and work/life balance offered may improve retention.

Accompanying these changes many firms have also planned long term changes in how work is staffed, and that is how, over a period of perhaps three or five years, they have improved their gearing. Others have concluded that they cannot make real progress because of their relatively small size and have merged, creating larger units better able to achieve higher levels of gearing.

It also raises the key question of what actually is the role of an equity partner? A question many would rather not ask! Is it to run files personally and to maximise their individual billing, or is it to run and manage a small team? The winners in the post-Clementi legal world are likely to be in the latter group. For many firms this will require a re-evaluation of the job of partner – a potentially difficult and sensitive task.

In these firms a partner may still have some clients and will still spend part of their time on client work, but the actual work they do may well be different. Their cases may be more complex and they may spend more of their time supervising and training more junior lawyers. They may be responsible for a team generating fees of, say, £750,000 rather than simply a personal caseload of, say, £150,000.

When considering gearing, firms also need to examine their methods of supervision and risk management procedures because those with high gearing require a very different role and contribution on the part of the partners, managers and supervisors. It is not simply a question of employing additional lawyers and carrying on with a largely unchanged workload yourself. Invariably the partners have to reduce their own caseload so as to create more time for managing and supervising others.

Quality standards such as Lexcel[1] can assist firms run well-geared practices in a risk-averse way because they require firms to consider both supervision and risk management, and to agree and document how these difficult areas are dealt with.

Revenue per equity partner

Another way of looking at gearing is to consider your firm's fees or revenue per equity partner. It is calculated by dividing the firm's headline revenue or fees[2] by the number of equity partners.

It is perhaps fairly obvious that a firm's actual level of fees – the total gross fees as shown in its accounts – is going to have a big impact on its profitability. Higher fees in themselves do not result in better profits, but if the financial structure of the firm is right they can.

Figure 11.4 shows the Law Management Section (LMS) Survey results for 2005, indicating that the most profitable firms were those with revenue per equity partner of around £900,000.

In Scotland the equivalent figure would have been fees per partner over approximately £350,000 to £400,000 – see Figure 11.5.

A similar picture is shown in respect of legal aid firms – see Figure 11.6.

All of these figures illustrate the same point – a key performance indicator (KPI) is revenue per equity partner.

Some of the larger firms, both in England and Wales and also in Scotland, have developed new 'bulk' areas of work that are high volume but low margin. Typically these departments employ very few qualified lawyers, use considerable amounts of IT, and can generate good profits – but at a low margin. If your firm does this type of work, this measure has to be treated with some care. You may like to calculate a figure for the 'non-volume' area of the firm and compare that with the charts.

Fees per equity partner is therefore an important KPI and one that all firms should be aware of. Firms that perform well may do so because their equity partners are high billers. It is more likely, however, to be related to

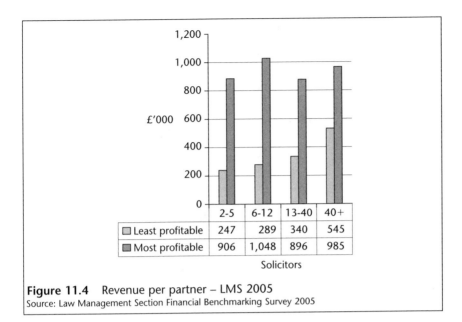

Figure 11.4   Revenue per partner – LMS 2005
Source: Law Management Section Financial Benchmarking Survey 2005

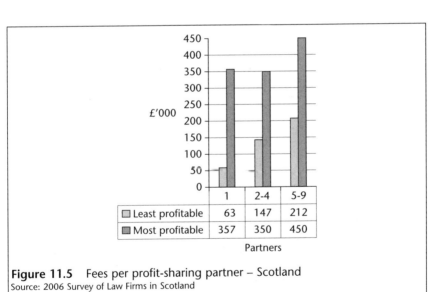

Figure 11.5   Fees per profit-sharing partner – Scotland
Source: 2006 Survey of Law Firms in Scotland

the number of lawyers they have in addition to each equity partner – their 'gearing' – and also the level of fees individual people bill. The latter will depend very much on the type of work they do, how hard they work and how good they are at billing.

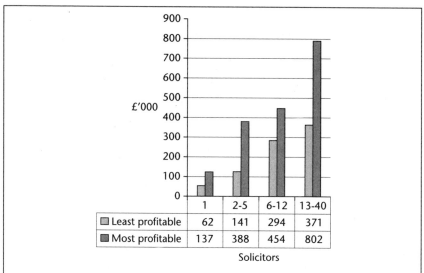

	1	2-5	6-12	13-40
Least profitable	62	141	294	371
Most profitable	137	388	454	802

Solicitors

Figure 11.6   Revenue per partner – legal aid firms – 2003
Source: DCA

SUMMARY

- Gearing is key to the profitability of many firms.
- Improvements to gearing can take several years to achieve.
- Key aspects of gearing are supervision, working methods and the role of a partner.
- A very useful related measure is revenue per equity partner.

Notes

1   The Law Society's practice management quality standard. A copy is included on the attached disk.
2   Traditionally interest earned on client account has been excluded from this calculation on the basis that, especially when interest rates were high, it was potentially dangerous for firms to become over-dependent on interest. Increasingly a good argument can be made, however, for including interest as for some areas of work, such as re-mortgage, the interest earned on client account is central to the viability of the work.

12

The main key performance indicators – salaries and overheads as a percentage of revenue

Net profit in the post-Clementi world

As discussed earlier, it can be difficult to assess and compare profitability in a firm of solicitors, and the measure often used in the past – net profit percentage – is not always a good indicator. In particular, if a firm has too many partners its salaries bill will be lower, its net profit percentage higher, but the actual profit per partner may not be as good, as illustrated in Table 12.1.

This difficulty in properly assessing the performance of a partnership is primarily because the profits the partners receive reflect their reward for contributions that in a corporate environment would be rewarded separately:

- the work they put into the firm as a lawyer or manager – **salary**;
- the capital they provide to help finance the firm – **interest**;
- the offices they own that the firm may occupy free of charge – **rent**;
- their risk as an owner – **profit**.

Table 12.1

£'000	Firm A	Firm B
Fees	2,000	2,000
Salaries	800	1,000
Overheads	600	600
Net profit	600	400
Net profit %	**30**	**20**
Number of partners	8	3
Profit per partner	75	133

A partner's profit share can, depending on the circumstances, in effect combine all of these – a salary, interest on capital, rent and a profit over and above these that justifies the risk of running the business.

In order more accurately to assess a firm's profits, therefore, it is necessary to make adjustment for three factors:

(a) a cost for each equity partner – a notional salary – to reflect his or her cost as a senior solicitor/manager working in the firm;
(b) a notional rent where the partners own their premises and are not charging the firm any, or a below market value, rent;
(c) notional interest on partner capital – something treated by most firms as a free source of finance.

Any balance left is the true profit of the firm.

Table 12.2 illustrates the point. The firm's fees were £8 million and its cost base was £5.5 million. Calculated traditionally this firm would have achieved a 31% net profit percentage. If allowance is made, however, for these 'hidden' costs, and the figures adjusted as if the partners had charged a market rate for themselves, for the offices they own and for the capital they have invested in the business, they make a net profit percentage of 11%. Perhaps most importantly, their cost base is now £7.2 million – 30% greater – and this is the 'true' cost of the firm.

One very likely result of the Legal Services Bill is that competition will increase, and margins will reduce – in which case firms will need to understand their 'real' cost base. Mistakes could easily be made if these other factors are not taken into account.

Table 12.2

	£'000	Unadjusted £'000	%	£'000	Adjusted £'000	%
Fees		8,000	100		8,000	100
Salaries	3,500			3,500		
Partner notional	0			1,000		
		3,500	44		4,500	56
Gross profit		4,500	56		3,500	44
Overheads	2,000			2,000		
Notional rent	0			300		
Notional interest	0			350		
		2,000	25		2,650	33
Net profit		**2,500**	**31**		**850**	**11**

Salaries as a percentage of fees

A firm's net profit is determined by the profitability of its people – its gross profit – and the level of its non-salary overheads. The two main key performance indicators (KPIs) for any firm are therefore salaries (having made allowance for an equity partner notional salary) relative to fees, and overheads (once again having made allowance for rent and interest) relative to fees.

The results from the Law Management Section (LMS) survey at Figure 12.1 indicate that on average, salaries (including a notional salary for each equity partner) were 65% of fees.

In the calculations in Figure 12.1 I have factored in a notional salary for each equity partner that varied with firm size. I used a salary of £60,000, £70,000, £80,000 and £90,000, respectively, for each of the four size categories – an amount intended to approximate the salary that might be paid to the highest paid employed solicitor in such a firm.

The second figure from the LMS survey, at Figure 12.2, indicates that amongst the most profitable firms salaries (including a notional salary for each equity partner) were around 50–60% of fees – or less.

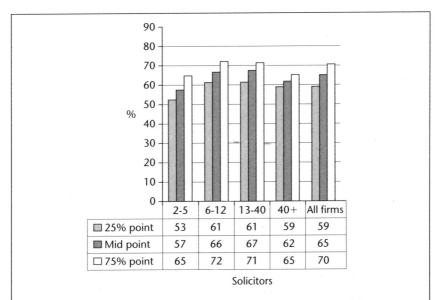

	2-5	6-12	13-40	40+	All firms
☐ 25% point	53	61	61	59	59
■ Mid point	57	66	67	62	65
☐ 75% point	65	72	71	65	70

Solicitors

Figure 12.1 Salaries (including partners) as a percentage of total fee income – LMS 2005
Source: Law Management Section Financial Benchmarking Survey 2005

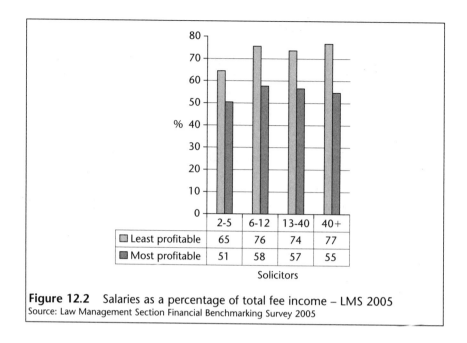

Figure 12.2   Salaries as a percentage of total fee income – LMS 2005
Source: Law Management Section Financial Benchmarking Survey 2005

Figure 12.3 indicates that for firms in Scotland the most profitable firms were those with salaries as a percentage of fees of under 50% – using a notional salary of £66,000.

Overheads as a percentage of fees

Figure 12.4 indicates that amongst the most profitable LMS firms, overheads – excluding all salary costs – were approximately 30%.

In this figure an allowance has been made for interest on partner capital.[1] No adjustment could be made for a notional rent as that information had not been asked for in the questionnaire.

Figure 12.5 indicates that in Scotland, amongst the most profitable firms overheads were around 25–30%.

In the Law Society of Scotland survey, firms were asked whether they owned their offices, and whether a market rent was paid. They were also asked for details of partner capital, so adjustment could be made for both a notional rent and notional interest.

To summarise the various statistics in this chapter, the profile of the most successful firms at present in England and Wales appears to be one where salaries, including a notional salary, are approximately 55% of fees, or less. Non-salary overheads are under 30%, leaving a net profit, after having paid the partners a notional salary, of approximately 15%.

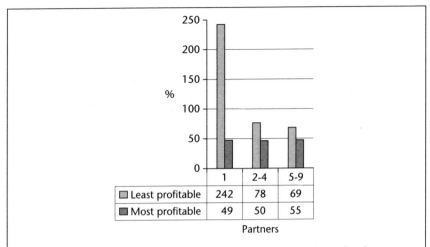

Figure 12.3   Salaries as a percentage of total fee income – Scotland
Source: 2006 Survey of Law Firms in Scotland

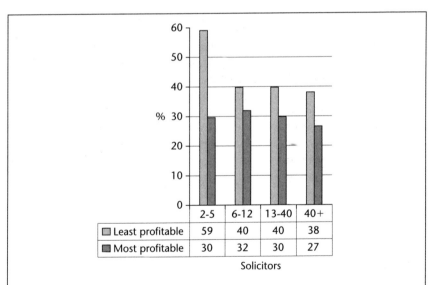

Figure 12.4   Non-salary overheads as a percentage of total fee income –
LMS 2005
Source: Law Management Section Financial Benchmarking Survey 2005

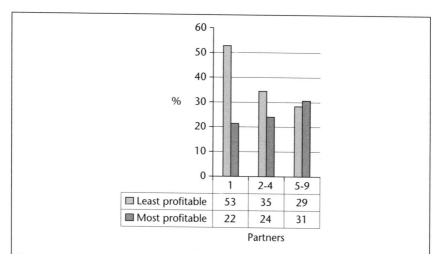

Figure 12.5 Non-salary overheads as a percentage of total fee income –
Scotland
Source: 2006 Survey of Law Firms in Scotland

SUMMARY

- In order properly to assess performance in a partnership,
  adjustment should be made for:
    - a notional salary for each equity partner;
    - a notional rent where the partners own the firm's offices and
      a market rent is not charged;
    - interest on partner capital account.
- The two main KPIs are salaries and overheads relative to fees.
- The profile of the more profitable firms in England and Wales
  would appear to be one where salaries are less than 55% of fees,
  and overheads less than 30%.

Note

1   At a rate of 7.5%.

13

Team profitability

Some principles

The key to improving profitability is to understand and monitor the performance of your lawyers, and the teams they work in.

Many firms have historically assessed performance by looking at the fees individual lawyers, or 'fee earners', billed. Many still use this today – it is often the key figure the partners look at. Simply looking at the fees of an individual or team is not, however, the same as assessing their profitability.

The main problems are that very often lawyers who achieve high personal fees – especially partners – need high levels of support staff in order to function. They also often run departments with poor gearing. The work is frequently technically complex, or perhaps they are simply poor delegators, but often high billers have few if any other lawyers working with them. By the time the cost of their secretaries, their share of a firm's overheads and their profit shares (which are often high) are taken into account, there is often little profit left.

Monitoring performance by reference to individual fees can also be highly detrimental to any attempt to change working methods, in particular any attempt to work on a team basis. People will hang on to work they should have passed to someone more junior, or to someone more specialised, if they feel they are in any way being judged by the fees they bill. The position is even worse if they are paid a bonus related to individual fees.

This emphasis on simply monitoring fees has been used by some firms almost as a proxy for management. In particular, when the partners are themselves busy working on client matters, the one thing they are normally short of is time. A monthly report of individual fees provides a quick way for them to gauge performance. From such a report it is easy to spot the lawyers that are doing well and those that are struggling. High fees are assumed to be 'good' and the lawyer with high fees is praised and rewarded. The difficulty is that it is sometimes the high biller who is the real problem – the partner or senior lawyer who keeps all the best cases and fails to delegate or feed his team with work. Insecurity is a common problem amongst many professionals, and this need for high personal fees and the recognition they bring also brings security. An added problem with reporting individual fees outside a department or team can be that partners in other departments, who may not even know the individuals concerned, can make judgements about them based simply on the fees they bill. They make a judgement without understanding the actual work the person does or their contribution to the team.

There is obviously a need to monitor fee income, however simply monitoring each person's fees does not provide a full picture of what is happening. If you are going to look at fees it is probably far better to look at departmental or team fees and find other ways to assess individual performance. It is even better to try to assess the profitability of the teams.

Unfortunately, assessing team performance is itself not easy. There are several reasons for this, but perhaps the main ones are as follows:

- Lawyers do not always work exclusively in one area of work. Say a solicitor spends 75% of her time on conveyancing and 25% on probate. What do you do? Put 75% of her salary cost into conveyancing, and 25% into probate? What about her secretary? Very quickly it becomes complicated.
- It is not clear how you should treat equity partners. If the solicitor had been an equity partner would any cost have been included at all? Or are partners a 'free resource', who simply receive a share of the profits?
- It is not clear what you should do with overheads. In order to show the total cost of a department it is necessary to spread the firm's overheads across them, however any allocation is going to be arbitrary, and the analysis can easily become complicated.

The example below is not un-typical, but illustrates the problems that can arise. It is an extract from an Excel spreadsheet that contained nearly 50 lines of overheads analysed over the firm's various teams. It was an attempt to assess the profitability of their teams. It contained nearly 600 figures over two pages of small print, but did little to explain the lack of profitability of the firm.

	CLIN NEG & PI	Probate	Crime	Housing
FEE INCOME				
FEE INCOME	368,927	120,984	180,651	313,147
PARTNERS' EMOLUMENTS	6,989	0	0	337
OTHER INCOME				
BANK INTEREST RECEIVED	7,280	0	0	0
OTHER INCOME	180	24	109	453
	7,387	24	109	453
TOTAL INCOME	**383,303**	**121,008**	**180,760**	**313,937**
OVERHEAD EXPENSES				
ADMINISTRATION				
ARCHIVE COSTS	852	269	462	747
BOOKS/MAGAZINES	149	77	101	262
BOOKS/MAGS (SUBSCRIBED)	5,404	611	496	829
STATIONERY	3,011	993	1,698	2,640
PHOTOCOPYING CHARGES	818	271	460	716
POST & DX	3,774	1,210	2,084	3,314
	14,008	**3,431**	**5,301**	**8,508**
COMMUNICATION				
TELEPHONE & FAX CHARGES	4,090	1,345	2,273	3,561
TELEPHONE MAINTENANCE	395	132	223	344
	4,485	**1,478**	**2,496**	**3,905**
COMPUTER				
COMPUTER HARDWARE (NON-CAP)	1,957	580	1,025	1,693

Un-picking salaries

Although many firms have found it quite difficult to assess team profitability, it can actually be relatively easy to produce something that provides a pretty clear indication of what is happening. The key is to keep the figures simple, to avoid complexity and to focus on the figures that are directly related to the teams or departments concerned.

Chapter 12 set out two main key performance indicators (KPIs) – salaries and overheads as a percentage of fees, and indicated that the former was *the* key figure to focus on. This comprises two elements:

- the salaries of the people in your teams or departments;
- the salaries of the people that work in central departments such as accounts, reception, etc.

In Chapter 12 the charts from the Law Management Section (LMS) survey indicated that overall salaries, including a notional salary for each equity partner, were approximately 65% fees, and amongst the most profitable firms, the level was around 50–60%, or less.

Figure 13.1 indicates that central salaries[1] are typically around 8% of fees. Amongst the most profitable firms, central salaries are approximately 7% of fees.

Table 13.1 indicates a simple model, in this case based upon the 13–40 solicitor firms from the LMS Survey. Figure 12.2 in Chapter 12 indicated that amongst the most profitable firms from this size group, salaries were around 57% of fees. In other words, a gross profit of 43% was being achieved towards overheads, central salaries and a 'real' profit for the equity partners.

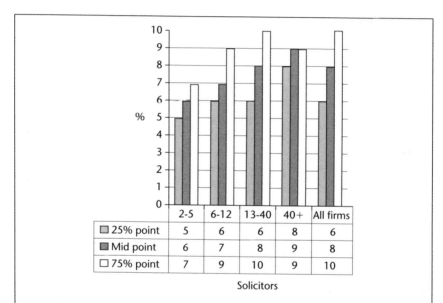

	2-5	6-12	13-40	40+	All firms
▨ 25% point	5	6	6	8	6
▦ Mid point	6	7	8	9	8
☐ 75% point	7	9	10	9	10

Solicitors

Figure 13.1   Central salaries as a percentage of total fee income – LMS 2005
Source: Law Management Section Financial Benchmarking Survey 2005

Table 13.1   Example: 13–40 solicitor firms (LMS Survey)

	%
Fees	100
Salaries	57
Gross profit – before overheads	43

If central salaries are assumed to be approximately 7% amongst these firms, departmental salaries would have been approximately 50% as indicated in Table 13.2. In other words, a typical department, with fees of, say, £1 million would have achieved a profit, before central staff costs and overheads of £0.5 million.

A well performing department should therefore be achieving a departmental profit percentage of approximately 50%.

Assessing team profitability – a simple methodology

The starting point in assessing performance is to determine what your departments or teams actually are.

Firms with more than, say, a dozen lawyers are likely to be structured into reasonably clearly organised departments – only that department will undertake that work type, it will have a range of precedents and appropriate supervision will be in place. Lawyers in other departments will not dabble!

In smaller firms, in particular in rural locations, the opposite becomes the norm, with individual lawyers undertaking a range of work that could include conveyancing, probate, crime, personal injury and family. In these situations it can be difficult to assess the profitability of different areas of work. It may be possible to assess the performance of different people, however in a small practice in particular, this can become divisive.

There will be a range of firms between these two positions, and the underlying principle has to be to keep it simple. In particular, avoid splitting people across departments. In the example described earlier, of the conveyancing lawyer who also undertakes some probate, it is much easier to put all of her fees and salary costs into conveyancing, her main department. You are assessing the performance of her and her colleagues.

Having determined your teams or departments, the next stage is to decide which figures can usefully be allocated:

Table 13.2   Example: 13–40 solicitor firms (LMS Survey)

	%
Fees	100
Departmental salaries	50
Departmental profit	50
Central salaries	7
Gross profit – before overheads	43

1. **Fees** – It is relatively easy to allocate fees across the various teams. Once you have decided which lawyer is in each team you can allocate fees accurately between teams. Put all of a lawyer's fees and costs into the same team – avoid the temptation to split people.

2. **Lawyer and support staff salaries** – It is also easy to charge each team with the cost of the people that work in it – the various lawyers, secretaries and other support staff who work directly in that team. Remember to include a notional salary for each equity partner working in the team, as well as employers' national insurance contributions (NIC), pension contributions and other attributable salary costs such as temps and locums.

3. **Interest on client account** – Traditionally interest would not be allocated to individual teams on the basis that in the past this has actually formed a significant part of the profits earned, and it would have been dangerous to assume it was going to continue, in particular when interest rates were high. Interest received would, therefore, be shown as a deduction from overheads. There is a good argument nowadays, however, that for certain areas of work – re-mortgage is one example – the interest earned on client account is a key component of the viability of the work, that can be expected to continue, and should be credited to the team.

4. **Departmental overheads** – There will be certain overheads which are within the control of the team or departmental head which can be usefully allocated to the team. Examples could include training, marketing (in particular the substantial advertising expenditure that personal injury departments can incur) and cost draftsman charges. They relate to the team, and should be charged to the team.

5. **General overheads** – Traditionally, as in the example above, firms have allocated all their overheads – rent, audit, telephones, light and heat – across the various departments. Little is gained by this allocation, indeed much can be lost as all the argument and debate at a partner meeting can be dissipated on discussing the basis of allocation – rather than the real factors that affect the profitability of different areas of work. Many managing partners, however, have argued strongly that it is only when overheads have been allocated, and a departmental loss has arisen, that their colleagues will pay attention and recognise there is a problem. Politically, therefore, there may be advantages to allocating general overheads – provided everyone's attention is then directed at the items that are within the control of the departments, i.e. their salaries, direct overheads and their fees.

6. **Volume department overheads** – In recent years many firms have opened volume or bulk departments, sometimes in separate buildings or on different floors. They are frequently clearly separate and have clearly identifiable costs. Because the margins are often slim, and because the risks can be much higher, it is important that the true

cost of these departments is known, and all the direct, attributable overheads are allocated. Within general overheads where there are additional items such as rent and other costs that are attributable to these departments, it can be useful to identify them and charge them to the departments concerned.

7. **Central salaries** – Some firms 'lose' central salaries within a single salaries line that is allocated across the departments. It is far better to show central salaries separately from departmental salaries, and as in the case of general overheads, little is to be gained by allocation apart perhaps as a device to draw attention to a problem.

Table 13.3 illustrates this approach. It shows the profitability of each department before any allocation of general overheads or central salaries has been made, and illustrates the relative lack of profitability in residential conveyancing. This department comprises 35 lawyers – over one-third the firm's total, and is the least profitable department. The issues to be discussed are likely to centre on:

- the fees that can be charged – although these will be to a large extent determined by the market;

Table 13.3   Team profitability example

	Commercial £'000	Residential property £'000	Private client £'000	Litigation £'000	Total £'000
Fees	1,500	2,000	1,000	3,500	8,000
Salaries	520	810	210	1,160	2,700
Partner notional	200	267	199	267	933
Dept. overheads	25	15	7	125	1/2
	745	1,092	416	1,552	3,805
Gross profit	755	908	584	1,948	4,195
%	50%	45%	56%	56%	52%
Central salaries					800
Partner notional*					67
Overheads					1,828
Notional rent					300
Notional interest					350
					3,345
Net profit					850
Lawyers	8	35	8	44	95
Equity partners	3	4	3	4	15
* Managing partner					

- the mix of staff in the department and numbers of staff;
- use of technology, working methods and systems generally.

The department is also top heavy with equity partners – it has four. That is likely to be a highly sensitive issue and one that the four conveyancing partners may wish to avoid discussing. It is likely, however, to be central to the issue of profitability.

Table 13.4 shows the same analysis but with an allocation of general overheads and central salaries. I have allocated these pro rata to the number of lawyers, and, because residential conveyancing has a large number of lawyers they have been allocated £1.2 million, resulting in a loss for the department. This loss does highlight that there is a problem, and will make it much more difficult to avoid a discussion on the issue. The risk is that the discussion will focus around the basis of allocation – if a different method (for example, floor space occupied) had been used, the result might have been different.

Table 13.4

	Commercial £'000	Residential property £'000	Private client £'000	Litigation £'000	Total £'000
Fees	1,500	2,000	1,000	3,500	8,000
Salaries	520	810	210	1,160	2,700
Partner notional	200	267	199	267	933
Dept. overheads	25	15	7	125	172
	745	1,092	416	1,552	3,805
Gross profit	755	908	584	1,948	4,195
%	50%	45%	56%	56%	52%
Central salaries					800
Partner notional*					67
Overheads					1,828
Notional rent					300
Notional interest					350
	282	1,232	282	1,549	3,345
Net profit	473	−324	302	399	850
Equity partners	3	4	3	4	15
Lawyers	8	35	8	44	95

* Managing partner

There are plenty of firms that have got lost in arguments like this, around the allocation assumptions, that have never then moved on to discuss the real issues of the underlying profitability of the department. The key, therefore, is to only use allocation as a notional calculation, something indicative of the position, and then focus attention back to the real issues – the items within the control of the departments.

Benchmarks

Figure 13.2 illustrates a wide range in departmental profitability[2] for the firms in the LMS Survey 2005. It indicates, perhaps as would be expected, that crime and family were least profitable. It also indicates that across each worktype some firms are achieving departmental profit percentages in excess of 50%.

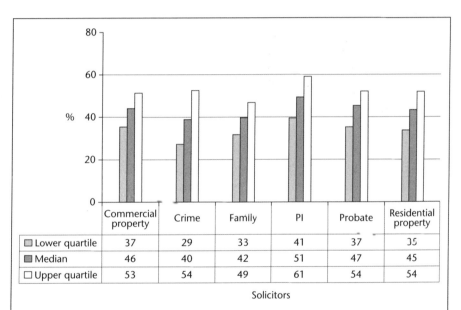

	Commercial property	Crime	Family	PI	Probate	Residential property
Lower quartile	37	29	33	41	37	35
Median	46	40	42	51	47	45
Upper quartile	53	54	49	61	54	54

Solicitors

Figure 13.2   Departmental profit as a percentage of fees – LMS 2005
Source: Law Management Section Financial Benchmarking Survey 2005

SUMMARY

- In order to assess performance, individual fees billed is of very limited value – it is far better to try to assess the profitability of teams or departments.
- When assessing departmental performance, avoid complication – also only analyse those items that are actually within the control of the departments concerned.
- It can be useful to allocate general overheads, but this should only be done as a tool to highlight problems. It must always be remembered that the figures that result are very dependent on the assumptions used. They are not necessarily correct or true. The key figure is departmental profitability before any allocation of general overheads.

Notes

1   No allowance has been made for time spent by the equity partners on management. In practice if, for example, the managing partner spends half of her time on management, half of her notional salary should be included with central salaries rather than being charged to her department.
2   This chart must be treated with extreme care due to uncertainty regarding the reliability of some of the data provided.

14

Understanding your firm's cost base

Calculating hourly cost

As competition increases due to the Legal Services Bill it is going to become ever more important that firms understand their cost base. In particular, if they have to enter price competitive tenders it is important that they understand the cost of their work.

There has been a trend in recent years to move away from pricing work on a time basis, in particular for commercial work, however it is still necessary to know what your work has cost. You need to know whether you have made a profit.

As any accountant will know, costing is a complex area that can be debated and argued about for hours – marginal cost, fully absorbed cost, variable cost, fixed cost etc. It is very easy to be overwhelmed by the jargon, and the resulting calculations and concepts can be complicated. This chapter discusses a couple of relatively simple ideas to help firms assess the cost of their time, and to compare it with other firms.

For many years the Law Society published a booklet called *The Expense of Time*,[1] and in Scotland the equivalent booklet was called *The Cost of Time*. *The Expense of Time* was a relatively complex methodology, written to reflect changing costs during periods of high inflation, however in essence it is a very useful starting point in calculating hourly cost, and in setting prices. The methodology set out here is fairly simple by comparison, but hopefully is one most firms should be able to follow, and perhaps more importantly, that most partners should be able to understand.

Taking the firm in Chapter 12 (at Table 12.2) as an example, its total cost base was just under £7.2 million, including partner notional salaries, rent and interest. If we calculate the firm's capacity – the number of hours of work its lawyers are going to produce and get paid for – we can divide one into the other and calculate an overall hourly cost: a single figure that reflects a number of underlying factors that provides a very useful benchmark for comparison to other practices.

Capacity

A law firm is selling many things – its expertise, its knowledge, its skill – but its service is provided in units of time. You may not charge the client on a time basis, but in measuring the cost of the work you need to know how long you have spent on the matter. When trying to calculate cost it is necessary, therefore, to establish how much time you are going to sell – in other words, what is your firm's capacity?

In *The Expense of Time*, the Law Society assumed that an average lawyer would produce and sell 1,100 chargeable hours of time a year. Some would do more, some less, but on average 1,100 hours was considered reasonable. In *The Cost of Time*, the Law Society of Scotland assumes 1,000 hours a year for a partner, 800 hours for trainees and 1,200 hours for all other lawyers. The lower partner figure reflects partners' need to spend part of their time on management.

In the 2003 survey of legal aid firms undertaken for the DCA, 137 firms provided details of the chargeable hours produced by their lawyers. The partners were producing around 1,300 hours a year, and the other solicitors approximately 1,200.

In a survey published in 2006 as part of Lord Carter's Review of Legal Aid Procurement,[2] solicitor chargeable hours amongst the leading crime firms averaged 1,500 a year.

In establishing your firm's capacity you should ideally use sensible actual figures for your own lawyers. In the absence of these, averages could be applied from other sources, such as an appropriate survey.

Taking the example firm used in Chapter 12, Table 14.1 calculates the firm's capacity on the basis of the Law Society of Scotland guidelines of 1,000 hours for partners, 800 for trainees, and 1,200 for all other lawyers; the assumptions are summarised in Table 14.2. These are probably more realistic for most firms than the 1,100 hours from the Law Society of England and Wales, which is arguably rather out of date now.

In this example, the firm has a capacity of 106,000 hours a year.

Table 14.1   Capacity

	Number	Assumed hours	Capacity
Equity partner	15	1,000	15,000
Salaried partner	5	1,000	5,000
Solicitor	45	1,200	54,000
Other qualified lawyers	10	1,200	12,000
Unqualified	10	1,200	12,000
Trainees	10	800	8,000
	95		106,000

Table 14.2 Average cost per hour

	£'000	£'000
Salaries	3,500	
Partner notional	1,000	
		4,500
Overheads	2,000	
Notional rent	300	
Notional interest	350	
		2,650
Total		7,150
Capacity		106,000 hours
Average cost per hour		£67

Figure 14.1 calculates an average cost per hour for each of the firms in the LMS Survey 2005, and an overall median of £92 is indicated. The example firm does well against this benchmark, as its average of £67 an hour is below the lower quartile.

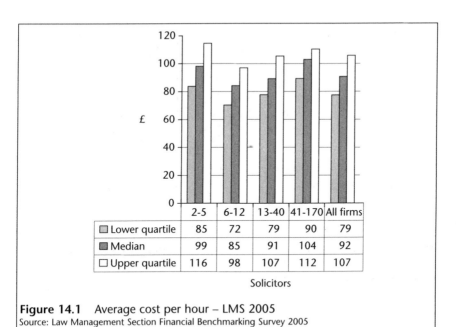

Solicitors	2-5	6-12	13-40	41-170	All firms
Lower quartile	85	72	79	90	79
Median	99	85	91	104	92
Upper quartile	116	98	107	112	107

Figure 14.1 Average cost per hour – LMS 2005
Source: Law Management Section Financial Benchmarking Survey 2005

Figure 14.1 assumes:

Firm size – number of solicitors	Equity partner notional salary		Chargeable hours assumed
2–5	60,000	Equity partners	1,000
6–12	70,000	Salaried partners	1,000
13–40	80,000	Associates and assistants	1,200
41–170	90,000	Trainees	800
		Other fee earners	1,200

These calculations are highly sensitive to the number of hours people are assumed to work, and, as a matter of interest, Figure 14.2 illustrates the hourly rates if the higher chargeable hours found amongst the large crime firms in Lord Carter's review were used, and indicates a median of £77 an hour.

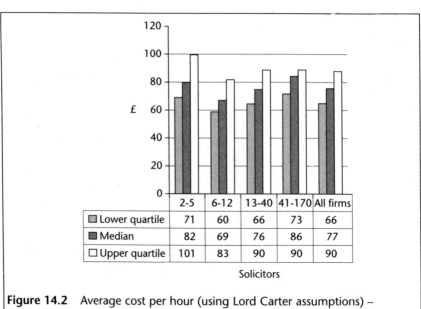

	2-5	6-12	13-40	41-170	All firms
Lower quartile	71	60	66	73	66
Median	82	69	76	86	77
Upper quartile	101	83	90	90	90

Solicitors

Figure 14.2 Average cost per hour (using Lord Carter assumptions) – LMS 2005
Source: Law Management Section Financial Benchmarking Survey 2005

Figure 14.2 assumes:

Firm size – number of solicitors	Equity partner notional salary	Chargeable hours assumed	
2–5	60,000	Equity partners	1,000
6–12	70,000	Salaried partners	1,500
13–40	80,000	Associates and assistants	1,500
41–170	90,000	Trainees	1,200
		Other fee earners	1,400

Achieving lower average cost

Some areas of work are likely to become highly price competitive as a result of the Legal Services Bill. Residential conveyancing is cited as one area in particular that may be attractive to new market entrants.

For firms that undertake work in these areas of greater competition – and residential conveyancing is important for many practices – it is likely that those with the lowest cost base will be the ones that will be best able to compete and survive.

Although relatively few firms undertake publicly funded work today, the review by Lord Carter provided an interesting analysis of the drivers of lower cost in an area of law that is already subject to intense price pressure. This was based on a survey of 38 of the largest crime firms in England and Wales.

Table 14.3 indicates that in this survey the firms achieved a median cost of £52.60 an hour, but that in a quarter of cases firms achieved an average of less than £45.44 an hour.

Table 14.3   Average cost per hour – major crime firms

Fee earners	Based on the median hours of all the firms			
	Cost/hour Median £	Cost/hour Lower quartile £	Cost/hour Upper quartile £	Fees/hour £
13–40				
Median	53.24	43.46	60.24	51.37
Mean	57.54			58.98
40+				
Median	52.50	47.14	59.90	57.27
Mean	55.37			59.46
All				
Median	52.60	45.44	59.90	53.07
Mean	56.51			59.21
Source: Lord Carter's Review of Legal Aid Procurement				

Table 14.3 assumes:

Firm size – number of fee earners	Equity partner notional salary	Chargeable hours assumed	
13–40	61,723	Equity partners	1,000
41–170	68,703	Salaried partners	1,500
		Associates and assistants	1,500
		Trainees	1,200
		Other fee earners	1,400

Table 14.4 examines the firms in this survey with the highest and lowest hourly cost. Those that achieved the lowest hourly cost were those:

- with fewer qualified lawyers – 57% compared with 75%;
- that were focused – in the case of this group of publicly funded firms those that specialised in legal aid and in crime achieved the lowest hourly cost;
- that had higher levels of gearing;
- that achieved higher levels of chargeable hours;
- that had lower overheads per lawyer – £13,000 compared to £29,000.

Overheads per lawyer

A very useful figure to be aware of, and to calculate for your own firm, is overheads per lawyer. Table 14.4 indicates that the lowest cost crime firms achieved a figure of just £13,000 per lawyer. The example firm in this chapter had total overheads of £2,650,000 and 95 lawyers – £27,900 per lawyer. Once again, in a highly competitive market firms that are able to spread their overheads over a larger number of lawyers, so that the overheads per lawyer are £13,000, or perhaps less, are likely to be the winners.

Figure 14.3 shows overheads per lawyer from the LMS survey and indicates an overall average of £33,000.

Conclusion

The issues posed in this chapter will provide some firms with real challenges. The position will vary according to the area of work firms practice in, however generally, as price competition increases, firms will need to understand their cost base much better in order to remain competitive.

In essence, the winners will be those firms that are able to process higher volumes of work relative to their cost base resulting in a lower unit cost. The losers will be those providing services in a more traditional way, quite possibly to a very high standard, to clients who are no longer willing to pay the fees that result.

Table 14.4 The drivers of lower cost – major crime firms

Cost per hour	Number of firms	Average Cost £p	Total Fee earner	% fee earn qualified	Fees £'000	Crime fees £'000	Public % %	Crime % %	Solicitor Chargeable hours	Gearing	Overheads fee earner £'000
Below lower quartile cost per hour	10										
Median		40.81	29	57	1,772	1,649	100	98	1833	9	13
Mean		40.20	39	60	2,302	1,835	94	84	1907	16	14
Below median cost per hour	9										
Median		48.30	37	54	2,700	2,700	98	98	1550	11	20
Mean		48.75	51	56	3,585	2,899	88	84	1739	17	20
Above median cost per hour	9										
Median		55.81	28	60	2,300	2,000	99	90	1500	7	17
Mean		55.80	59	59	4,799	1,979	78	75	1653	10	20
Above upper quartile cost per hour	10										
Median		75.76	33	75	3,944	1,408	57	35	1350	5	29
Mean		80.44	40	76	4,351	1,711	55	38	1432	7	36
All	38										
Median		52.60	34	60	2,611	1,772	95	86	1500	9	20
Mean		56.51	47	63	3,736	2,089	78	70	1668	12	23

Note – the actual chargeable hours supplied by each firm were not used to calculate the average cost for that firm. They were used to calculate averages which were applied across all firms.

Source: Lord Carter's Review of Legal Aid Procurement

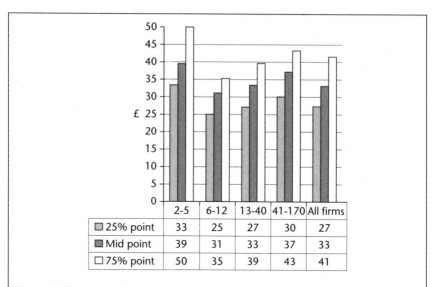

	2-5	6-12	13-40	41-170	All firms
25% point	33	25	27	30	27
Mid point	39	31	33	37	33
75% point	50	35	39	43	41

Figure 14.3   Non-salary overheads per lawyer – LMS 2005
Source: Law Management Section Financial Benchmarking Survey 2005

SUMMARY

- The Legal Services Bill is likely to result in competition from new entrants to the market, and the consequence will be downward pressure on fees.
- In order to survive, firms will need to have a clear understanding of their cost base, and in particular their overall cost per hour.
- A key component of cost is capacity and, although firms may not charge on a time basis, they need to maintain reliable information on how many hours lawyers are achieving – they need to continue time recording.
- A useful figure to be aware of and to calculate for your firm is overheads per lawyer – for some firms this figure will be below £13,000 a year, in other instances it is over £50,000. In an increasingly price competitive market the winners are likely to be firms where this figure is relatively low – they have a large number of lawyers to spread their overheads over.

Notes

1   Now out of print.
2   See **www.legalaidprocurementreview.gov.uk**; Otterburn Legal Consulting Analysis of FreshMinds solicitor survey 2005 and subsequent research 2006.

15

Budgets

Budgets continue to be a very useful tool for improving long-term profitability because they translate the aspirations and somewhat intangible nature of a business plan into something more concrete. The problem is that in many firms it is a mechanical exercise in which the opportunity to consider key issues is missed.

Budgets have traditionally been prepared for 12-month periods, and are used subsequently during the year to compare to actual. Whilst this is essentially the correct way to use a budget, care must be taken with too much focus simply on this 12-month period. The firm will, hopefully, continue after the end of the 12-month period and too much focus on this '12-month snapshot' can make you lose sight of the longer-term picture. A 'rolling' budget can be a very helpful concept and this is discussed later in this chapter.

When?

The best time to prepare a budget is in the final two months of the financial year, when the outcome for the coming year can be seen with some certainty.

Who?

The way *not* to prepare a budget is for the finance director or accountant to do it on his or her own, spending hours closeted with a complex Excel spreadsheet! The process needs to be led by your finance staff but must involve heads of department, team leaders and fee earners, especially when considering fee levels and the amount of working capital each team should be working towards.

How?

Budgets comprise four elements:

- fees;
- salaries;
- overheads;
- working capital.

Of these four areas, it is normally relatively easy to predict what a firm's overheads and salaries are going to be. Setting the fees budget is normally the most difficult, or at least it can appear so – in reality this also is not normally too difficult.

Fees

When considering the fees budget it is usually useful to look at past performance – the fees of each fee earner or department or team, perhaps for the last three years. You need to involve the fee earners concerned, they have to feel able to 'buy into' the budget, but it is always best if you can start the discussion with a first draft set of figures – an indication of the level of fees you expect the team to produce.

It is very useful if fee levels can be justified by looking at the hours you expect each person to achieve or the number of matters you expect them or their team to complete in a period.

An illustration of a fees budget based on chargeable time is illustrated in Table 15.1 for a six-partner firm, but the principles would be the same for working out a budget for a department within a firm.

The starting point for this fees budget is the total time you expect each person to be in the office, and the proportion of that time that you expect will be chargeable. I have assumed that most fee earners work seven-hour days, but that partners work 10-hour days. In reality most partners work at least 10-hour days, and this is probably repeated across the professions – most self-employed people tend to work relatively long hours.

I have then made an assumption about the number of chargeable hours each level of fee earner is expected to achieve, and this could be confirmed by looking at the actual chargeable hours your fee earners achieved last year. In this case five hours a day has been assumed for partners, five-and-a-half for other solicitors and four-and-a-half for paralegals. Some firms, especially those doing legal aid, would assume higher targets than these and might expect fee earners to achieve six or six-and-a-half chargeable hours a day. You must be very sure such levels are achievable within your own firm before basing a budget on such high levels. It is better to budget for something less ambitious and then beat it, rather than be too optimistic in your budgeting.

Table 15.1   Fees budget

	Total hours per day	Total annual hours	Chargeable hours per day	Annual chargeable hours	Hourly rate £	Total potential fees £	Assume 80% recovery £
Partner 1	10	2,300	5	1,150	140	161,000	128,800
Partner 2	10	2,300	5	1,150	140	161,000	128,800
Partner 3	10	2,300	5	1,150	120	138,000	110,400
Partner 4	10	2,300	5	1,150	120	138,000	110,400
Partner 5	10	2,300	5	1,150	75	86,250	69,000
Partner 6	10	2,300	5	1,150	75	86,250	69,000
Solicitor 1	7	1,610	5½	1,265	110	139,150	111,320
Solicitor 2	7	1,610	5½	1,265	110	139,150	111,320
Solicitor 3	7	1,610	5½	1,265	110	139,150	111,320
Solicitor 4	Assume no fees this year – starts half way through year						0
Paralegal 1	7	1,610	4½	1,035	70	72,450	57,960
Paralegal 2	7	1,610	4½	1,035	70	72,450	57,960
							1,066,280

The average hourly rate could be the fee earner's quoted charge out rate, or a better figure to use could be the actual average the fee earner is currently achieving. This is calculated by taking the fee earner's fees – say, for the last three months – and dividing this by the number of chargeable hours recorded. You may then wish to increase the hourly rate to take into account any projected increase in fee rates planned.

This is a good opportunity to review the hourly rates each person charges. It is surprising how many solicitors charge relatively low hourly rates that do not fully take account of their ability or market rates. There is sometimes a reluctance to ask a rate people feel could be challenged. To a degree, however, quality is often judged, at least initially, by the rate you quote. To be too low does not help if, in reality, you are one of the leading lawyers in your area for your area of work.

As a matter of prudence the totals have then been reduced by 20%. This is a safety margin to allow for a fee earner not achieving either the chargeable hours or the average rate. In particular, fee earners may not always be able to bill all the time recorded on a matter – they do not achieve a 100% recovery – and this makes allowance for this potential shortfall.

This fees budget straightaway raises a number of issues, which should be challenged before the budget is finalised, such as:

- How many hours do we expect each person actually to be in the office?
- How should the partners use their time?

- How many chargeable hours do we expect each fee earner to achieve each day?

The latter in particular requires careful consideration of what each person actually does. It may be, for example, that the paralegals have low chargeable hours because they take on non-chargeable administrative work, especially in the case of some areas of legal aid, freeing others to achieve higher fees.

The fees budget includes a solicitor due to start half-way through the year. This person may, depending on the work they do, generate fees in their first six months, but they may not. In this example, a cautious approach has been adopted and it has been assumed they will not generate any fees in this financial year.

When operating in a fixed-fee environment quite different considerations can apply, and the budget is once again a very useful tool in prompting the partners to consider issues such as:

- working methods;
- the level at which work is done;
- supervision.

The key questions are, how many matters should a team complete in a period, and what fee will the firm be paid for each? The key figure to monitor quickly becomes the number actually completed.

Salaries

The salaries budget, by contrast to the fees budget, is relatively straightforward. The starting point is your current headcount and each person's current salary. You then need to add any additional staff planned for the coming year, and also take account of any expected salary changes. Finally you need to allow for employers' national insurance contributions (NIC), as illustrated in Table 15.2.

This example includes an allowance for a notional salary for each equity partner. This has been included so as to allow the budget to be assessed against the various benchmarks set out earlier in this part.

Overheads

The final stage in preparing the budget is to consider the overheads of the firm. Most people simply take last year's actual and add a percentage to allow for inflation. This is a useful starting point, but is not the best way to prepare an overheads budget. It is far better to work through each line and consider each individually.

Table 15.2 Salaries budget

	£
Solicitor 1	45,000
Solicitor 2	35,000
Solicitor 3	28,000
Paralegal 1	18,000
Paralegal 2	16,000
Secretaries (×4)	60,000
	202,000
Pay review – 5% half way through year	5,000
New solicitor – at £25,000 for six months	12,500
	219,500
NIC (say 12%)	26,300
	245,800
Partners – 6 × £60,000	360,000
	605,800

Start with the major items, such as rent and business rates, professional indemnity insurance and depreciation. These three alone will account for a significant proportion of your firm's overheads, and should not take long to calculate. With the exception of professional indemnity insurance, they are likely to be relatively fixed and you will already know how much to budget.

Of the remaining items, some will apply to the whole firm – such as stationery, telephones, most library expenditure and insurance – but there will be a small number that are specific to particular departments. These will include some marketing (but not firm-wide items such as Yellow Pages), some library (but not the main subscriptions that are firm-wide) and some training. It is a good idea to let each department set a budget for these items and for them to identify their proposed expenditure in these areas – and they should prepare schedules itemising what they intend to spend their budgets on.

When considering the central overheads it is worth spending time looking at each item and asking what the expenditure was on, was it required and did you obtain value for money? One approach is known as 'zero-based budgeting' – which literally means that you start with a budget of zero for each item and then justify each pound. Obviously a reasonably broad-brush approach has to be adopted, but this can be a good way of challenging expenditure and obtaining better value. Do not be afraid to put certain areas periodically out to tender, such as insurance, stationery and accountancy and audit. The latter in particular is an area of great variation. Some firms of accountants charge remarkably high fees for a relatively limited, reactive service.

In the case of the example firm, the overall overheads budget was finalised at £297,000 – a reduction of 3% on the previous year. Table 15.3 summarises the overall budget and indicates a projected profit of £163,000. After adding-back the partner notional salaries, this should provide a profit per equity partner of £87,000.

The percentages in Table 15.3 can then be compared to the benchmarks earlier in this part to assess how the firm is budgeted to perform.

In practice firms can produce several drafts of the budget before it is agreed, and the process can take several weeks. In industry the whole concept and value of budgeting has been challenged in recent years because of the time required and the limited impact the process actually can have in large organisations. The process has become an annual chore, especially for the accounts department, rather than something that adds value.

In most professional firms budgets are still a very useful tool because they force firms to think about their income and expenditure, however firms should guard against the process just becoming routine. It has to add value.

Working capital

Having completed the profit and loss (P&L) budget, it is very useful to complete the process and set targets for working capital, in terms of work in progress (WIP), disbursements and outstanding debtors. This should ideally be worked out on a departmental basis as illustrated in Table 15.4. The starting point is to calculate an amount per fee earner that can then be worked-up into an overall target for the department.

Table 15.3   Overall budget

	%	£'000
Fees	100	1,066
Salaries	46	606
Overheads	28	297
Budgeted net profit	26	163

Table 15.4   Working capital budget

	Target per fee earner (based on historic data for the firm)	£'000
Residential conveyancing (3 fee earners)		
WIP	15,000	45,000
Disbursements	1,500	4,500
Outstanding debtors	5,000	15,000
Family (4 fee earners)		
WIP	25,000	100,000
Disbursements	1,800	7,200
Outstanding debtors	13,000	52,000
Crime (2 fee earners)		
WIP	5,000	10,000
Disbursements	1,800	3,600
Outstanding debtors	5,300	10,600
Commercial (2 fee earners)		
WIP	30,000	60,000
Disbursements	1,300	2,600
Outstanding debtors	19,000	38,000
		348,500

12-month or rolling?

As discussed at the start of this chapter, budgets are usually prepared for a 12-month period. This is generally very helpful, because the financial year provides a timescale against which progress can be assessed. In many firms one of the biggest problems is getting fee earners to give billing the priority it deserves, and the discipline of annual, quarterly or monthly budgets is an essential stick in this process.

The main problem with this is that fee earners and partners can focus too much on these artificial 'accounting' periods and the year-end can be seen as the all-important deadline – whereas life actually continues afterwards!

It is very useful, therefore, in addition to the normal 12-month budget, to maintain a rolling 12-month forecast that looks further into the future. In effect you are 'pencilling in' another quarter at the end of the budget or the accounts to project current trends further into the future. This only needs to be prepared in outline – a fees figure, salaries and other overheads – possibly built up on a departmental basis, but it means you are better able to project the impact of what is currently happening in the market and to anticipate events earlier.

If your firm prepares accounts on a quarterly basis you would, as part of the accounts pack, include an extra page with an outline projection for the next nine months – the last three months plus the next nine projected. This will force people to be constantly looking ahead and will make people more alert to trends. For example, going into a slowdown in the economy, commercial firms may find it more difficult to achieve premium hourly rates, and fee earner utilisation, in terms of number of chargeable hours recorded, could fall. They may also find it difficult to achieve their normal charge out rates and the recovery of the time incurred on a matter may become more difficult. A normal budget or set of management accounts will not fully reflect the effect of this, whereas a rolling forecast will.

SUMMARY

- Budgets are a very effective extension to the business planning process because they translate the aspirations of the plan into something more tangible.
- The budgets should be led by the accounts department, but certain items (especially fees) need to be agreed at departmental level involving all fee earners.
- In addition to fees budgets, it is very useful to set budgets for chargeable time, WIP, debtors and unbilled disbursements.
- In addition to a 12-month budget, maintain a rolling forecast – three months actual plus nine months projected – so as better to assess what will happen in the future.

16

Information

The impact of information on behaviour

The information a firm distributes, in particular what is reported, and who receives it, can have a huge impact on behaviour, in particular the behaviour of its lawyers.

The one message that should come through clearly from the previous 15 chapters is that the profession is about to experience considerable change, and that most firms will have to evolve. In many cases this change will need to be radical if the firm is to survive and prosper.

Earlier chapters have discussed the importance of strategy and team-working. They have also discussed the role of leadership, and playing to the strengths of your people.

For many firms the hard part has always been actually translating these ideas into practice, and they have often not been helped by their financial reporting, in particular the information the partners look at each month. Their plans and aspirations have often been thwarted because the information the partners look at failed to evolve.

There are several problems, but perhaps the most important is the over-emphasis many firms continue to place on individual fees. The single most important report in many firms continues to be fees per lawyer or fee earner.

In many respects this type of report has been highly effective at achieving its main purpose – getting individual lawyers to maximise their personal billing. The problem is that in an environment where many firms need to move from a focus on the individual to a focus on the team, and when firms need to change their working methods, this particular measure starts to be counter-productive. Firms that continue to focus on individual fees, at the same time as trying to introduce teamworking, invariably struggle because their lawyers will continue to worry about their individual fees.

There is the same need for people to bill, but there is also a need for work to be delegated to more junior people, and for the role of those more senior to evolve – more supervision, more dealing with difficult matters, less simply fee earning. Thus different methods of assessing performance need to be developed.

An added difficulty is that by definition, financial reports only report things that can be easily measured and quantified. You may well be asking your partners to spend less time on client work themselves and more time supervising their team or marketing, but these are more difficult to quantify. New ways need to be found that set targets for these less easily measured areas, and then monitor what people actually achieve.

Many firms are also very secretive and can be wary of distributing information. Individual lawyers will be shown their own figures but rarely those of their colleagues or indeed the whole firm. There can sometimes be issues of confidentiality, especially in highly specialised fields or in small jurisdictions, but many lawyers are motivated by being shown how their team or the firm is performing. The gradual conversion of firms to LLP status has also had the effect of making them more open. When the fees of the firm, and indeed the profits, are open to public inspection the need for internal secrecy is lessened.

Areas to monitor

Perhaps the most obvious step forward for many firms will be to shift the focus from the individual to the team. Reports of the fees of each team and the profitability of the team, as described earlier in this section, are likely to be at the heart of most firms' financial reporting. Focus at this level, on the 'gross profitability' of each department, overcomes many of the difficulties of an individual focus and is likely to encourage change and delegation of work to the correct level.

A report showing the profitability of each team is one that in particular could be distributed amongst staff generally.

Within each team, however, there is also a need to monitor performance, and that may well include areas such as fees per lawyer, chargeable time per lawyer, time spent on marketing, supervision and administration, per lawyer. There will still have to be a focus on individual performance within the team, however because the prime focus will be on the team, the adverse impact on behaviour should be reduced.

Design and format of management reports

The design and format of management reports is very important. A few key points are:

- Keep them very simple – many lawyers simply do not like numbers; you need to make them easy to follow.
- Round figures to the nearest £'000.

- Where possible show previous quarters or years, as this helps comparison.
- Aim to produce management accounts as soon as possible after the period end and use estimates, as this will speed up their production.
- Use charts wherever possible, or perhaps a traffic-light system so as to help lawyers focus on the figures that need attention.

The problem in many firms is that the basic layout of their management accounts is poor. They are difficult to understand and it is hard to pick out the important figures.

EXAMPLE

Table 16.1 illustrates an example of a monthly accounts format, and many firms continue to produce something similar. The format is based on a set of annual accounts – the layout their accountants will be used to. The purpose of management accounts is different to that of annual accounts and this style of design has a number of flaws:

- The figures are to the nearest pound, and are therefore difficult to read.
- By simply showing the current period and year to date it is very difficult to get any idea of trends.
- There is too much emphasis on overheads – 24 lines in this case, compared to just one line for income.
- The more important performance ratios are not obvious

In this case, the key figures are fees – which are £150,000 below budget, and profits – with just four months to go, profits are nearly 25% below the level that had been hoped for.

Table 16.2 presents the same information in a very different format. These accounts are for November, which is mid-way through the third quarter. The first two quarters are shown in total and the actual results are shown for the first two months of this quarter together with a projection for December.

In this report less emphasis is placed on overheads – which are just shown as one line – and there is greater emphasis on the fees of the five departments. This highlights straightaway where the problems lie, and that some departments are actually ahead of budget.

Table 16.3 develops this format further and includes a notional salary for the equity partners. There are eight equity partners, and a notional salary of £40,000 has been used. The table highlights the collapse in profits in the second quarter to just £42,000. The projection for December and also for the final quarter have been revised and show the effect of the reduction in staff levels that are to occur in December.

The purpose of this format is to try to present the information in such a way as to highlight trends and focus management attention on the key figures. It is intended to get them thinking about what is likely to happen in the future, as well as analysing the past. You may well decide you want additional columns showing the actual variance – the difference between the budget and the actual – or alternatively you may want to remove some of the detail. The key is to highlight the information that is important to you.

Table 16.1   Smith & Co – Monthly management accounts

Smith & Co – Accounts – Period 8 – November				
	This period		Year to date	
	Budget	Actual	Budget	Actual
Fees	250,000	235,458	2,000,000	1,850,478
Interest receivable	2,000	1,758	16,000	14,569
	252,000	**237,216**	**2,016,000**	**1,865,047**
Salaries	95,000	96,785	760,000	775,852
Rent and rates	12,500	12,658	100,000	102,457
Light and heat	3,000	2,480	24,000	18,456
Telephone	5,000	3,254	40,000	36,741
Printing, stationery	4,500	5,521	36,000	29,963
Postage and DX	2,000	2,321	16,000	16,879
Professional indemnity	6,000	6,000	48,000	48,000
Other insurance	1,800	1,700	14,400	13,789
Repairs	2,000	1,563	16,000	13,258
Accountancy	1,500	1,500	12,000	12,000
Subscriptions	2,000	1,850	16,000	14,785
Library	2,000	2,245	16,000	14,587
Training	2,000	2,203	16,000	14,695
Marketing	2,000	1,756	16,000	17,458
Depreciation	7,500	7,500	60,000	60,000
Bad debts	2,000	1,458	16,000	14,789
Cleaning	750	745	6,000	5,895
Miscellaneous	3,000	2,896	24,000	22,458
Negligence claims	4,000	2,147	32,000	26,789
Bank charges	1,500	1,452	12,000	11,478
Bank interest	2,000	2,851	16,000	17,452
Motor and travel	1,800	2,504	14,400	17,825
Annuities (previous partners)	3,000	3,000	24,000	24,000
Practising certificates	2,500	2,500	20,000	20,000
	169,350	168,889	1,354,800	1,349,606
Profit	**82,650**	**68,327**	**661,200**	**515,441**

Table 16.2 Smith & Co – Quarterly accounts (revised format)

Smith & Co

Month 8 – November

£'000	Quarter 1 April–June		Quarter 2 July–September		October	November	December	Quarter 3 October–December Total	Budget	Year to date	Full year projection	Full year original budget
	Budget	Actual	Budget	Actual	Actual	Actual	Revised	Revised	Original	Actual	Revised	Original
Company commercial	250	220	250	126	86	79	65	230	250	511	796	1,000
Property	150	140	150	125	41	38	35	114	150	344	479	600
Employment	50	60	50	55	18	21	20	59	50	154	224	200
Litigation	200	210	200	212	72	68	70	210	200	562	832	800
Private client	100	105	100	110	35	29	30	94	100	279	409	400
Total fees	**750**	**735**	**750**	**628**	**252**	**235**	**220**	**707**	**750**	**1,850**	**2,740**	**3,000**
Interest	6	7	6	5	1	2	2	5	6	15	22	24
	756	**742**	**756**	**633**	**253**	**237**	**222**	**712**	**756**	**1,865**	**2,762**	**3,024**
Salaries and overheads	507	492	507	511	177	169	150	496	507	1,349	1,949	2,028
Profit	249	250	249	122	76	68	72	216	249	516	813	996

Table 16.3   Smith & Co – Quarterly accounts (revised format – incorporating notional salaries)

Smith & Co   Month 8 – November

£'000	Quarter 1 April–June		Quarter 2 July–September		Quarter 3 October–December					Year to date	Full year projection	Full year original budget
					October	November	December	Total	Budget			
	Budget	Actual	Budget	Actual	Actual	Actual	Revised	Revised	Original	Actual	Revised	Original
Company commercial	250	220	250	126	86	79	65	230	250	511	796	1,000
Property	150	140	150	125	41	38	35	114	150	344	479	600
Employment	50	60	50	55	18	21	20	59	50	154	224	200
Litigation	200	210	200	212	72	68	70	210	200	562	832	800
Private client	100	105	100	110	35	29	30	94	100	279	409	400
Total fees	**750**	**735**	**750**	**628**	**252**	**235**	**220**	**707**	**750**	**1,850**	**2,740**	**3,000**
Interest	6	7	6	5	1	2	2	5	6	15	22	24
	756	**742**	**756**	**633**	**253**	**237**	**222**	**712**	**756**	**1,865**	**2,762**	**3,024**
Salaries	285	289	285	291	99	97	75	271	285	776	1,076	1,140
Notional salary	80	80	80	80	27	27	26	80	80	214	320	320
	365	**369**	**365**	**371**	**126**	**124**	**101**	**351**	**365**	**990**	**1,396**	**1,460**
Gross profit	391	373	391	262	127	113	121	361	391	875	1,366	1,564
%	52	51	52	42	50	48	55	51	52	47	50	52
Overheads	222	203	222	220	78	72	75	225	222	573	873	888
Profit	169	170	169	42	49	41	46	136	169	302	493	676

Pro formas

The pro forma spreadsheets are included on the attached CD:

Overall reporting

Financial summary
Departmental profitability summary
Departmental profitability workings

Fees

Fees by team
Fees by fee earner

Management accounts

Quarterly accounts
Overheads
Balance sheet

Team reporting

Departmental or team report
Departmental or team accounts
Departmental or team summary
Individual fee earner report
Source of new matters

Cash

Cash plan

SUMMARY

- As firms evolve, develop team structures and change working methods, be aware that financial reporting also needs to evolve.
- An over-emphasis on individual fees can undermine attempts to change because lawyers continue to be protective of their own fees.
- The format adopted can have a huge impact on the value of a firm's management information.

17

Conclusion

Most firms in England and Wales are going to experience a period of significant change over the next five years from 2007 as a result of the Legal Services Bill. In the view of Professor Stephen Mayson, as many as a third may not survive.

The key areas to be aware of are the:

- need for effective financial control;
- importance of leadership;
- importance of line management;
- need for effective use of IT;
- need to challenge working methods;
- need for a plan.

The winners in five years' time are likely to:

- be larger – with at least 30 lawyers;
- have good levels of gearing;
- be working well in teams;
- be working in modern offices with good IT;
- have partners who have evolved their thinking and developed their roles.

There are many firms who are already doing all of this. They are ready for the challenge and are likely to prosper. The problem is that most firms are only just beginning to consider the issues. They will have much to do and relatively little time to do it in. The starting point is a recognition on the part of all the partners that they need to change, some courage and someone who will take the lead.

To manage successfully and develop, just being a good lawyer or great fee earner is not enough. The leaders of a modern law firm must embrace the best management practices and be prepared to inform and challenge themselves. If firms are to maximise their potential and maintain their competitive edge in a rapidly changing professional and social environment, they must adapt.

Further reading

Stephen Mayson, *Making Sense of Law Firms*, Blackstone Press 1997.

Robert Mowbray, *Maximising the Profitability of Law Firms*, Blackstone Press 1997.

David S Porter and Vanessa Openshaw, *Business Management for Solicitors*, Emis Professional Publishing 2001.

Heather Stewart, *Excellent Client Service*, Law Society Publishing 2003.

Simon Tupman, *Why Lawyers Should Eat Bananas*, Simon Tupman Presentations 2001.

Fiona Westwood, *Accelerated Best Practice: Implementing Success in Professional Firms*, Palgrave Macmillan 2004.

Index